Instant Networking

The simple way to build your business network and see results in just 6 months

Stefan Thomas

CAPSTONE
A Wiley Brand

Instant Networking

Contents

1
Why "instant" networking?

When people think of networking they often think of a room full of people introducing themselves to each other and going through the ritual of exchanging business cards. You probably picture everyone wearing a suit.

It's likely that expressions such as "elevator pitch" and "referrals" come to mind when you picture what networking looks like. It's likely that you think about shaking hands with lots of people and making small talk.

What networking *really* is though (for me at least) is a set of activities designed to grow one's personal network, add people to your address book, have more people that you can pick up the phone to and that isn't a cold call.

Networking events, in the small business, entrepreneur, professional and corporate world, are a huge part of the networking activities I refer to. But they are only one part of what networking actually means in the early part of the 21st century. There is a whole lot more that you can (and in my opinion should) be doing to accelerate the growth of your network and decrease the time it takes people to either decide to do business with you or consider you for a position in their organization.

I get asked all the time "what is the point of networking?" After all, at the time of publication in 2016, the online opportunities to promote oneself, not least through LinkedIn, Facebook, Twitter, Periscope, Blab, blogging and other platforms, are massive. But in my opinion, this is all part of the networking activities I referred to earlier. Networking is not just the semi-formal, ritualized exchange of the business card over breakfast. Networking is everything that you do to grow your network of contacts, while strengthening as many of those relationships as you can. Networking is the opportunity to take people who are on the very fringes of your network (for example, someone you have only met once at an event) and move that relationship forward to the extent that you trust each other and would do business with each other.

Networking, done right, speeds up the process by which people get to know, like and trust you.

Networking skills are for life, not just for breakfast

I sometimes think that a lot of people feel that networking is somehow separate to their other business activities. That the skills involved in networking aren't something you need to bother about unless you go to networking events. But I truly believe that the skills you develop in networking are essential in other parts of your career or business, and that networking is actually a pretty safe environment to develop those skills.

Much of what you do to either market your business or market yourself is designed to start a conversation.

When I was an estate agent, we advertised in the *Oxford Times* every week in order to try to start a conversation with the people who might want to buy or sell a house. Pre-internet the adverts were really an invitation for people to call us or call into our offices and talk to us.

Learning to get better at networking is actually about learning to get better at those conversations, and particularly how to engage and how to drive conversations if you want to do business with someone.

Learning to *be* better at networking is learning to *be* better at those conversations. You should actively set out to get better at networking, to sometimes use the networking environment counterintuitively and to use it in ways that other people don't. If you actively do that, you are also working on the skills that help you to improve your engagement, conversation and sales skills. Think about a very simplified sales process:

- You start a conversation
- You establish, either quickly or over time, whether the person may be interested in your services
- You introduce your services to them
- You ask them if they want to buy

Networking, used right, is a fantastic environment to learn, develop and hone these skills. Much of the value I have had from networking has been having the opportunity to

develop my sales technique and process in a safe environment, over a period of time.

I talk a lot about networking skills, and I wonder if people think that it doesn't apply to them, because they don't "go" networking. But it does. And they do.

You can't squeeze an onion online

Something that people ask me a lot is whether online networking and social media will mean that there is no need for face-to-face networking in the future. Whether business networking has, will or should move completely online.

I'm a member of lots of online forums and this question comes up very regularly: whether face-to-face networking is "dead" in a social world. Typically, it's a conversation I regularly start because I'm interested in people's opinions.

Overwhelmingly, people from all professions, trades and industries still choose to meet people. Despite all of the technological advances there have been, people still want to "press the flesh" and shake hands with someone before they do business with them; it seems as though we are hard-wired that way. In fact someone recently commented that if they absolutely can't meet one of their networking contacts, mainly due to geography, then they will Skype or FaceTime them. They went on to say that even in these instances, where they can be virtually in the same room with someone, it "just isn't as good" as physically being with them in person. Those small nuances of body language and facial

expression are lost even when we can see someone in glorious 1080p HD.

I try to explain the phenomenon to people, and then, out of the blue, a friend of mine called Martin Warrillow got talking about his shopping habits on Facebook.

To cut a long story short, Martin was asked why he doesn't do his grocery shopping online and his response was that his wife says that "you can't squeeze an onion online".

So what's the relationship between online onions and business networking?

You can achieve *so* much these days using social media and online marketing. You can assemble your crowd and create and nurture your prospects. You can research and engage with people you might want to do business with.

But you can't squeeze an onion online. For so many of us, what we sell needs us to have a relationship with our clients. Our clients need to have seen the whites of our eyes and got to know us a little bit before they are ready to do business. That feeling of knowing the person, rather than just the proposal, is what can often make the difference. That trust that comes from meeting someone in person and getting a "gut feel" for them makes every other conversation so much easier.

You might now decide to tweet me to tell me that you don't ever need to meet the people who buy your services or products, and you conduct all your business online. I completely accept that and how there are plenty of business models and businesses where you can sell a product or service directly to the consumer via a well-optimized online shop. I maintain though that there are plenty of businesses where you do need to squeeze the onion, where you do need to meet someone, shake their hand, have a coffee and get to know them before any business will progress.

Would you use an accountant or solicitor you didn't know and trust? And there are loads more professions and businesses where the same applies. Particularly those who give professional advice.

This is, to me, why business networking is such a shortcut. So much of our other marketing activity is designed to put us in the position where we are in direct contact with a prospect. Networking cuts straight to the point and puts you in touch with the people you want to meet straight away. Often sitting opposite them at a breakfast table where you have a chance to build the "warm" relationship before you move onto business.

But what if there aren't the right people in the room? I want to make sure I get straight to the decision makers!

When you prospect do you always get to the right person straight away? Or do you sometimes have a few wasted phone calls and even meetings first?

A networking environment puts you in the position where you can tell a lot of people about your business (advertise) and then actively target the people you want to speak to both in the room (in one to ones) and outside the room (referrals).

Network enough, and effectively enough, and you're giving people an opportunity to squeeze the onion before they buy it.

Is "instant" networking really possible?

So, is it possible then, or even desirable, to "instantly" improve your networking? Could you do stuff that would "instantly" make a difference?

Yes, I believe you can. I believe pretty much anyone can make changes and take actions right now that could result in a sale today, or at least move you much closer to making a sale today. Or maybe several sales. It depends on how much time and effort you choose to put in.

People do tell me, quite regularly, that networking doesn't "work", that they've tried it and it didn't work for their business. Sometimes even though there are plenty of people in the same business as them, who also go networking, it does "work" for them. So, we can take from this that there are some people who appear to be "better" at networking than others, maybe better than you feel you are.

I've had people say to me that they "tried" social media, but the return on investment wasn't good enough for them.

It's true that some of these relationships can be very long term, that the right opportunity just might not have been there yet. But it's also true that you can speed up the process whereby people trust you enough to do business with you or refer business to you.

In 4Networking that process is referred to as the **Meet–Like–Know–Trust** relationship. These are the inevitable steps that people take after they **Meet** you, they then decide whether they **Like** you or not (more on this later), then over time (or maybe a different measure) they get to **Know** you as the relationship deepens. Finally, they hopefully then decide whether they **Trust** you enough to part with their cash, or refer others to you to part with their cash.

In networking we talk about this process taking time. It is often thought that you have to wait for each part of the process to develop over time.

But I spent the first part of my career working in shops as a Saturday boy, and then a large part of my career as an estate agent and I learned how small changes in my behaviour or actions could have an instant impact on my results (sales). I have also spent time training retail staff and watching their results improve.

In the shops in which I worked, we had a very limited window of opportunity. From the moment someone walked into our shop, until the moment they left, we had to build that **Meet–Like–Know–Trust** relationship. Our ideal scenario was that they would come in with a desire to buy something and leave having bought that thing, and hopefully other things from us. We had the distinct advantage that they had chosen to come in, which showed they must have given some thought to buying something. It was then down to us to make sure that this happened and that we developed the trust (usually in less than 20 minutes), so that not only did they buy the products, but we could also suggest some other purchase – the skill of "upselling".

In my estate agency career, we would be asked to "value" a house or flat and very often the homeowner would invite several estate agents to do the same. Therefore, from the moment we knocked on their door, straightened our tie (yep, I did used to dress properly) and waited for the door to open, until the moment we left an hour later, we had to build the **Meet–Like–Know–Trust** relationship sufficiently, so that they would choose to give us their property to sell over and above the competition.

And some people were better at selling shoes, some people were better at upselling and some people were better at getting houses to sell than others.

Estate agents, retailers and most other businesses invest in training, because they understand that very often the sales performance of an individual can be improved if they make changes to how they work.

Putting it another way, an assistant in a shop, or a negotiator in an estate agency, can make instant improvements by making subtle changes to what they do in their day-to-day activity. Instant improvements that will immediately result in more sales and instant improvements that will build over time with application and practice. And it isn't just estate agency or retail; in any trade, business or profession, it is possible for the tradesperson, employee or professional to make subtle changes, which will have an instant impact.

And so can you and so can any business. So let's get on and do so.

2

Putting together your networking toolkit

Having the right kit is an essential part of speeding up the networking process. This chapter aims to help you assemble the correct tools in your toolkit to enable you to make the most of your networking journey.

Getting this stuff right, from the outset, will mean that you're not leaving things to chance and, when we investigate some further processes and structures later in the book, you will already be well prepared for them.

Having the right tools in place will also help you to feel more confident in your networking generally, knowing at every stage of the Meet–Like–Know–Trust process what you need to do next.

Putting structures into place also allows you to be more creative. Making a system for the actions you need to take, in pretty much the same order regularly, frees up your time, and thinking time, for the more important stuff.

The sales funnel myth

I come across far too many people who use networking to collect business cards and then don't really do anything with those cards afterwards.

If you are going to put effort into talking to people in the first place, it makes sense to ensure that as many of those people as possible are funnelled in the right direction and not just lost.

This is where the sales funnel comes in. You may be familiar with this concept, but if you're not, it works something like this.

In the kitchen, as you probably know, if you have a large amount of liquid to transfer into a container, you use the funnel to direct the liquid down into the right place, to avoid it spilling everywhere.

A sales funnel, then, is what you do to make sure that more of the people you first meet or engage with are directed into the right place. Specifically, if you are networking for the sake of your business, you may want to ensure that as many people as possible become customers or clients and don't spill out all over the place.

However, the reason I refer to it as the sales funnel *myth* is that I think that the use of a top-down funnel to illustrate the point is wrong.

To me, it gives the impression that the process is somehow gravity fed, much like the funnel itself. It gives the impression that if you put enough in the top, gravity will kick in and stuff (maybe sales or job opportunities) will magically appear out of the bottom.

For anyone who has launched a business and believed at first that that would be the case, you'll understand where I'm coming from. I did, I thought that if I collected lots of business cards, if I went to lots of networking events that **of course** some of these people will buy from me! I wonder how many of you readers have thought exactly that too?

In reality, I believe it is much more helpful to think of the sales funnel as lying on its side. Anything you put in will just sit there unless you do something to push or pull it through.

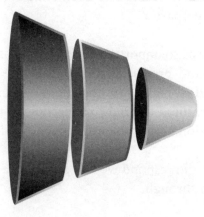

In business you have to create the engine that moves everything through your funnel. You need to either be the engine or create an engine. Particularly for small and micro businesses, often the owner of the business *is* the engine. As a business grows, it is possible to create an engine that will, in turn, enable the business to scale and grow.

Plan it – don't wing it

I'm not a natural planner. I can be pretty good at winging it and my speaking career, in large part, was down to my initial ability and willingness to step in when the proper speaker hadn't turned up and to come up with something convincing.

But winging it isn't a strategy. In any aspect of what you do in networking you really should plan.

In 20 years of advertising in the local newspaper as an estate agent, not once did we ever just wing it and bung some stuff in there because we hadn't had time to, or hadn't bothered to, prepare.

That advert was so important to us, particularly in the days pre-internet and pre-social media, that we had to get it right. We had to make sure that the advert said the right things and featured the right properties, so that it started the conversation and people responded.

When people did respond we had a system, a structure, for moving them through.

If you walk into a shop and express interest in a product, the sales staff will (or at least should) then have a system for helping you to move through the process of choosing and then purchasing the right product for you.

Despite appearances, very few successful businesses would wing it or leave that process to chance. Even the most apparently laid-back businesses will have structure in the background that allows them to appear relaxed.

Preparing some systems and structures, as early as possible, will also allow your business to grow, because you won't need to reinvent the wheel every time you add someone to the funnel.

Your networking introduction – a vital part of your toolkit

At the majority of networking events (those that I have attended at least) you will have the opportunity to introduce yourself and your business to the people assembled in the room.

This is generally called the introductions round, or, more commonly, the 40-second round, or 60-second round. The titles will give you a clue as to how much time you are allowed to speak for!

If that doesn't sound like enough time to get your message across, bear in mind that most TV adverts are around 30 seconds long. It isn't about how long you have, but how you use it!

It's crucial then to have something prepared in advance, at any networking event, which is going to achieve a number of things:

1. It will help you to feel more confident, something that is important to a lot of people, including me. If you prepare and practise enough, you will have less to worry about on the day.
2. It will help you to understand where your introduction fits into your overall networking strategy and structure.

In my opinion, your introduction is one of the methods you use to bring people into your network, to add them into the funnel. Your 40-second or 60-second introduction can be one of your ways of starting the conversation with others.

It helps to have some planned introductions so that, if required at a networking event, you can present confidently without trying to "wing it" and come up with something to say as you stand up.

It also helps to have a selection of introductions so that you can change the introduction to suit the audience or, as I do, to connect with particular people in the audience who you would like to talk to. (I talk about an audience in the broadest sense of the word; at a typical networking event there are likely to be anything from 12 to 30 people there.)

Think about your introduction in the same way you would an advert in the newspaper or your window display if you owned a shop. The point is to draw people in, to encourage people to want to find out more. The point is *not* to give away so much so that people feel they can tick the box and don't need to speak to you any further.

I believe that if you consider your introduction less as a broadcast and more as the beginning of a conversation, then you will find it easier and are likely to attract more people to you.

There are a number of ways to structure your introduction (ok, there are unlimited ways, but I will focus on just a few here). To some extent the structure will depend on the type of networking meeting you are at (whether you are pitching for referrals for your business or sales for your business).

In order to plan your introduction, consider the following:

What problem do you solve?
What has one of your clients said about your product or service?
What do you love about your work?

It is worth really studying the above and observing if certain words stand out. Emotive words really help to convey your message.

Think specifically about what your audience are buying, not what you're selling. The difference is subtle, but crucial.

You may well have heard the following advice in other sales or marketing training or advice you have taken but it particularly holds true in networking: when you plan any message you need to think and speak in terms of the benefits of your service and not the features.

A **feature** is something the product or service has. A **benefit** is something it does.

If you are at all unsure, apply the "so what?" test to anything you are about to include in your introduction. If you were to say it, and someone were to say "so what?", what would you say next? And what if someone said "so what?" to that as well, then what would you say?

(Please note that at a real-life networking meeting *nobody* is going to say "so what?"; they wouldn't be that impolite! This is simply your way of getting to the real crux of your message.)

Also, try to build on any point you make with the expression *which means that...*

Some examples of features and benefits:

> Feature – we've been established since 1997.
> Benefit – we have almost 20 years' experience, *which means that* whatever you need doing, we have massive experience in doing it for other clients, *which means that* we can be efficient *and* we know the pitfalls other providers may miss at first, *which means that* our solution will be excellent value for money and do the job you intended it to do.
> Feature – we have seven fully qualified members of staff.
> Benefit – I have a large and expert team behind me, *which means that* if I am ever not available, any of my team

can pick up your query straight away, *which means that* you are never kept hanging on, even if I am out networking!

Feature – Our offices are on the Old Station Road Business Park outside town.

Benefit – We've positioned ourselves in modern offices, *which means that* you can visit us easily because we have free parking, *which means that* if you ever want to check on the progress of your project you are welcome to call in for a coffee (nobody will, but people love the idea that you are visible).

Think hard about what that feature actually means to your prospective customers or clients and turn it into language that will help them to understand that.

People have often said to me "but it's difficult to sell coaching/consultancy/training courses (add your own as appropriate)". That's because that isn't what people want to buy.

When someone goes into a store to buy a spade, they don't want a spade. They want a hole.

When someone buys paracetamol they don't want a painkiller. They want rid of their headache.

Nobody wants sales training, it's expensive and time consuming! But what they do want is to make more sales.

Nobody wants an accountant. But they do want to pay as little tax as possible and make sure their business stays the right side of the various laws and regulations.

Nobody wants a coach. But they do want to feel in control of their life.

If you can sum up exactly what people will achieve by working with you, you will make massive progress.

An introduction to sell "to" the room

At a networking event where you are there to promote your business to the others in the room, the six-part structure detailed below has proven a very effective way of getting your message across:

1. This is who I am
2. This is what I do
3. This is how I do it
4. This is what someone else has said about me
5. This is what you need to do next
6. This is who I am

So you only have six things to remember and plan for.

1. This is who I am

First, tell people, clearly, who you are and what your company or business is called. This also helps people to tune into your voice. It also, subtly, builds some immediate trust because it is what people are expecting to hear.

2. This is what I do

Then tell people what you do. Think in terms of the benefits I talked about above.

3. This is how I do it

Explain, concisely, how you do it. Think about using words and phrases that really bring it to life for the people listening. For example, instead of saying you run training courses, explain that you run "fast-paced training courses designed to give you the maximum benefit in just five hours". Don't say that you coach people; explain that "my clients spend six weeks working with me intensively to improve their sales/life/business planning".

4. This is what someone else has said about me

Give people a testimonial somebody has left for you. If someone has left a testimonial for you on LinkedIn, or has emailed you commenting on your service, take the opportunity to ask them if you may use that elsewhere and do so. In networking circles, this may well be someone that other people know, so it further establishes the trust.

5. This is what you need to do next

Explain what someone needs to do next if they want to find out more. Commonly referred to as a "call to action" this helps people to understand what to do next and, subtly, gives them permission to do just that. Don't ever presume people will know what to do next. If you are at an event that encourages one to one conversations in group time, such as 4Networking, then invite people to ask you for a one to one. If you want to direct people to your website or leaflets, then give them the details. If your goal is to get people to sign up for your newsletter, then explain how they can do so.

6. This is who I am

Remind people who you are because they may not have been listening first time round. They aren't being rude, but in a networking meeting with lots of people speaking at different volumes, it may have taken someone a few moments to "tune in" to your voice. Giving them your name again at the end helps anyone who does want to ask you for more information, or for a one to one.

An introduction to sell "through" the room

If you are at a networking event where the point of the introduction is to ask for referrals, then you simply replace the "call to action" with your referral request, so the structure looks like this:

1. This is who I am
2. This is what I do
3. This is how I do it
4. This is what someone else has said about me
5. These are the types of referrals I am looking for
6. This is who I am

When asking for referrals, specificity is important. Try to be as specific as you possibly can.

Think of it like this:

- If I ask you to think of anyone who owns a house, that's too many people.
- If I ask you to think of someone who owns a three-bedroomed house, you can think of someone but don't know if that is who I really mean.

- If I ask you to think of someone who owns a three-bedroomed semi-detached house in the older part of town with a driveway and garage and preferably a privet hedge in the front garden, you think "oh yeah, John". And that is *exactly* the response you want when asking for referrals. You don't want to be so broad that your request could apply to someone's entire address book. You want to be so specific so that even if only one person in the room can think of someone, it is *exactly* the right person they are thinking of.

Be specific about the business, about the business name, even about the business person you would like to be introduced to, if you can be that specific.

There are a few pitfalls that can easily be avoided during the introductions round, with just a little thought and preparation.

When I was very young and being trained in sales, I was told that if you don't like where a conversation might go, don't start the conversation; if you don't like one of the possible answers to a question, don't ask the question. My advice about introduction pitfalls pretty much goes along with that advice.

Saying "we have just launched our business" or "we are just about to launch our business". Bear in mind you are telling people that you are very new to this. Most people aren't early adopters by choice. Most people would prefer to wait until a few more people have tried your service out before they jump in. You don't need to draw attention to it, just tell people what you do. Some may ask how long you've been doing it, and in a one to one conversation you can give a fuller answer, but don't deny yourself the chance to at least have that conversation.

Along similar lines, saying "I wear different hats" or finishing describing one service and then saying "and we also do this" can give the impression that you're not really committed to "the other thing". There is an English expression that I hope translates everywhere else. It refers to someone being "Jack of all trades and master of none". If you possibly can, work out how you describe both services as one, or choose to lead on one and introduce your other services to people once you are talking to them.

At every stage, remember that you are starting a conversation. Make sure you are talking your listeners into that conversation and not out of it.

Have a system to follow up

Your introduction should start the conversation. Taking my "sales funnel" analogy further, your introduction is your opportunity to add people to the funnel, to build your network.

What you do next is crucial to your networking success, and having a system in place as early as possible for what you do next is important.

I choose to use a CRM (customer relationship management) system to help me record, in detail, all of my networking contacts and to plan, again in detail, what next steps I should take.

There are very many CRM systems on the market and which one you should use will be largely a matter of personal preference, budget and relevance to your industry or profession, because some CRMs specifically aim themselves at certain market sectors.

You might choose to use a paper system, or another software system outside of the CRM description, but whatever you do, put a system in place.

What a system will do, specifically, is ensure that you remember every single opportunity that pops up because, guess what? You've got a busy life and if you don't record things you will forget them.

It also helps you to fulfil the little promises you make, because the little promises help to build trust with the people you meet along the way.

A system that I use and that works very well for me is to record every single contact I make at networking events and then plan some follow-up. I am going to talk about follow-up in detail in Chapter 6 but for now make sure you have a system of some description, and my recommendation would be a decent CRM.

I personally use Capsule CRM (I have no affiliation with Capsule, I just love their product) and thoroughly endorse their system for its simplicity and integration with other systems.

A social footprint

Once again, I'll be covering social in much more detail later, but for now you need people to be able to find you. Because social is where people connect, it makes it easy to keep in touch and simple to build those relationships.

There are thousands of social media platforms now. If you're not already, you need to be on LinkedIn, Facebook and Twitter at the very least. I'm not overstating it by saying you need to be on those platforms. There are others that you could probably be on, but those three are a necessity.

The world of networking *has* changed over the years and today a lot of your networking will be conducted online. When I wrote *Business Networking For Dummies* in 2014 I was used to comments at networking events that social media was unnecessary or "just all hype". I was still coming across people who were not convinced of the value of social media in "real" business relationships, but now it is absolutely vital.

This is where you will build the searchable footprint for your personal brand, whether that is as a business owner or someone with a corporate career.

Business literature

It really is worth having, at the very least, some business cards as you embark on your networking journey, or step it up.

Even now, because so many people store everything electronically, the exchange of business cards is important and is still the universally accepted way of giving someone your contact information.

Investing in a decent quality business card still does say a lot about your business. I know there are companies out there who offer free business cards. Don't cheapen your own personal brand with these. Getting decent quality cards costs next to nothing and makes a statement that you're investing in yourself and your business.

Please do consider that a *lot* of people now scan business cards straight into their CRM. Bear that in mind when having your cards designed. I tend to scan cards and then dispose of them, and on my networking travels there are a lot of people who do the same.

With this little lot, you should be set. Even if you have been networking for years, you may not have everything in place. Do it, set yourself up for winning more business from networking.

3
Thinking differently about networking

Of course networking doesn't just "work".

Now there's a surprising comment from me. But it comes from a comment I spotted somewhere, where someone was questioning whether anyone "really gets any business from networking".

My problem with this statement is that it suggests that networking is just an activity. That if you simply turn up, something will magically happen. You go along, do your 40 seconds, talk to some people and people will buy from you, just because you're a member of the same club.

Networking, like anything else in business, rewards effort. And networking, in and of itself, doesn't deliver business. But it does deliver something else.

Networking delivers opportunities.

This, I think, is one of the most misunderstood aspects of any sort of business networking, including social media. Instead of delivering sales, networking delivers a number of opportunities, and it's your job to make the most of each of them. These opportunities include:

- **Some business people in the same room** – business people need to buy services. It's an opportunity to be there among people who might want to buy your services.
- **Presenting your business in the introductions round** – you've got a load of business people in front of you, and now you've got the chance to give them the opportunity to find out more, by exciting them in the 40-second round.
- **One to one meetings** – the opportunity to have a warm conversation with other business people, instead of making cold calls.
- **Something in common** – this is a huge unfair advantage. You are starting any conversation at a networking event and you already have something in common with the person you're speaking to.
- **Warm follow-ups** – once again, you don't need to make a cold call. You've shared coffee, breakfast and a conversation with the person already.
- **A ready-made social media following** – you do connect with everyone you meet on social media don't you? Please tell me you do. Whatever their preference is, whether it's LinkedIn, Facebook, Twitter, Instagram or anywhere else, you have the chance to connect with them.
- **Improve your public speaking** – presenting your "stuff" one to one or to a room full of people does set many business people apart. Being able to speak about your business and your expertise opens up even more opportunities, and, in my experience, actually helps you to feel more confident.

- **Bringing value to your relationships first** – giving referrals and leads to other people is a huge opportunity to be the first to deliver value – and is made even easier when you've had the chance to learn about other people's businesses, by listening to them.

There are more; I suspect someone will tell me in the comments about what I've missed, in their opinion.

The most successful networkers look for, and actively work for, the opportunities rather than waiting for the business to come to them.

Aim to be interested rather than interesting

Dale Carnegie, in his 1937 book *How to Win Friends and Influence People*, said: "You can make more friends in two months by becoming interested in other people, than you can in two years by trying to get other people interested in you."

Think for a second about why you go to any networking meeting. Do you go for the sake of your business? Do you go because you hope that ultimately networking will lead to more sales for you?

You bought this book, I presume, because you wanted to sell more stuff at networking events? Or progress your career by using networking?

Now here's the thing: everyone is the same as you.

Everyone else arrived at the networking meeting this morning or this evening for the sake of their business.

You're the only one who arrived for the sake of *your* business.

So guess what? There is only one person in the room interested in your business and that's you.

This is a massive change of approach for most people, because we seem to think that what we need to do is have a clever "elevator pitch", that we need to talk to people, as soon as possible and as fully as possible, about what we do in our business.

But everyone else is interested in their stuff first. So start by being interested in them, in your early conversations, in your one to one meetings. Find out as much as you can about them and be patient. When the time is right they will talk to you about your business, but let them tell you all about theirs.

People often ask me how to move on from the small talk to the "real" conversation. Remember though that the small talk *is* the big talk. Those little social conversations are the glue that holds the relationship together. Those little things in common, shared interests, support for the same sports team. All of these things make a huge difference to how much people feel they "know" you and trust you.

Make sure when you do so, that you listen. Listen properly. Actually allow your mind to process what they're saying.

Most people don't actually listen. When others are talking, most people spend their time processing what their reply will be, or thinking about how they can use this as an opportunity to sell. Just listen and be genuinely interested.

It's ok not to be confident

I haven't mentioned confidence as such so far, because I think we get very hung up on it.

There are some really simple ways you can feel and appear more confident at networking meetings:

- Get to know the other attendees on social media *before* the event, then you will have people you already know to talk to.
- Prepare what you're going to say before you get there.
- Talk to the organizers on the phone when you book in, so that you are familiar with the format and how the meeting works.
- Be yourself; don't try to pretend to be something else, or put on a cloak, it's much more difficult to keep up the pretence if you're not feeling it.

And, most importantly, don't get too hung up on it. You know what? It's ok to be nervous about doing something new, or about being in a new environment. Roll with it; don't worry about it (because you've got enough to worry about anyway!). Everyone is nervous at first and the people in the room who appear the most confident are probably very nervous inside.

Be proud of yourself for going out of your comfort zone. Others will be supportive of you for doing so.

How to be "in the right place at the right time"

I am told very often that I was "just in the right place at the right time".

People have said to me, even to my face, that I "just got lucky".

When I was approached to write my first book, I just happened to be there, in the right place at the right time. I just happened to be at that event, that night, in east London, where there was also a commissioning editor present for the *For Dummies* series of books, and we struck up a conversation.

When I was asked to be the annual keynote speaker for The Business Networking Show in the UK, it was because I just happened to be there and happened to know the organizers.

When I was asked to speak at The Content Marketing Academy in Edinburgh, alongside some of the world's leading authorities on content, it was because I just got lucky and got to know the right person.

Here's the thing about that. Since 2007 I've been to over 1,000 networking events, I've made a huge and consistent effort to meet as many people as possible and to keep in touch with as many of those people as I possibly can.

I've got up at 4am many times and driven through the night many times to get to, or home from, networking events. I've chosen to network online instead of watching television (except for *Doctor Who* and the rugby, obviously) and even when I do watch television, I take part in the online chat too, building and strengthening my network that way.

Being in the right place at the right time is surprisingly simple. It's just not that easy. You have a much better chance of being in the right place at the right time if you're in more places than anyone else, more of the time.

Let's take The Content Marketing Academy and how I ended up being "lucky" and speaking there.

In 2007 I joined 4Networking and decided to throw myself at their online forum as well as their real-life networking.

Sometime in 2008 someone mentioned this guy called Gary Vaynerchuk on the 4Networking forum and I decided I liked his stuff and started watching his YouTube videos. I also bought his first book *Crush It*.

In December 2013 Gary was making a rare visit to the UK and speaking in London, so I bought tickets and went along. The event was promoted with the hashtag #vaynerworld.

After the event I set up a Google Alert so that if anyone wrote anything about the event, I would get an email alerting me.

Scott Torrance, who had also attended the event (but whom at this point I had never met), blogged about #vaynerworld on the blogging platform Medium. I liked his blog post, so commented and then shared it on my social media channels, tagging Scott as I did so.

Scott and I got into a conversation on Twitter.

I needed to go to Edinburgh for some other business, which is where Scott was based at the time, so I made sure I made time to have coffee with him while I was up there. It was time to "squeeze the onion".

After a while he decided he liked my stuff enough to invite me onto his podcast to talk about business networking. (The podcast still exists on my blog.)

We kept in touch and he shared with me a white paper he produced about networking for one of his clients, which I still share from my blog.

During this time I continued to go to hundreds of networking events and wrote my first book *Business Networking For Dummies*.

Scott then asked if I would have time to take part in a podcast for a friend of his, Chris Marr, who is the founder of The Content Marketing Academy. At this point Chris and I had never met.

I spoke to Chris on Twitter and then on the phone and was flattered to appear on his very popular podcast (once again, still available on my blog).

Chris and I keep in touch and I became part of his very vibrant Facebook group.

That was in December 2014, a year or so after I had first engaged with Scott and I needed to go to Glasgow for a networking event, which is only an hour or so drive for Chris, so we organized to have dinner.

Over dinner Chris asked if I would like to be part of his event and so in September 2015 I was thrilled to be a keynote speaker at his flagship event in Edinburgh.

The story doesn't actually end there. As a result of implementing what I learned at The Content Marketing Academy and building that into my networking routine, I have now been presented with another, even larger, international opportunity.

All of the effort in all of this was front loaded. I was in the right place at the right time because I was on the 4Networking forum, then at Gary Vaynerchuk's event, then on Scott Torrance's blog, then on Twitter, then in Edinburgh, then on his podcast, then out networking even more, then on social some more, then on Chris Marr's podcast, then in Glasgow.

And so on and so forth.

I do believe in the principles of working smart. I really do. But I also think that hard work – good, old-fashioned graft – is massively underrated.

I *have* been in the right place at the right time, much more often than other people, because I furiously and religiously put myself in as many places as I possibly can, as much as I possibly can.

I'm not telling you this story to big myself up. I'm telling you this story because I have many other stories just like this. How I got to write the first book. How I got to speak in the places I am now "lucky" enough to be invited to. How I got invited to write this book. And so on.

If you really want this, if you really want to grow your business or your career then by all means work smart. I often think that a whole load of other people work a lot smarter than me.

But don't ever think that working smart is a substitute for working hard. Effort is currency, particularly in social media and networking relationships. Being the person who is seen more, who is in contact more with other people, who is visible more of the time. That effort is rewarded.

My constant strategy is to build my network as wide as possible, while getting as close as possible to all of the people I meet.

It is incredibly important to constantly add people to your network and here's why.

If you think of your network as a series of concentric circles, people often enter your network right at the outside. If you think about how I "met" Scott Torrance, it was because he posted a blog about an event we had both attended. At that stage, when I liked and commented on his blog, we didn't "know" each other, let alone "like" or "trust" each other. For sure, Scott had made a start on that process by writing a decent blog, as had I by taking the time to read it and letting him know that I had.

And over time, Scott and I moved closer to each other. In my set of concentric circles, Scott moved quickly from right at the outer edge, to really close to the middle. That was the sweet spot when we ended up doing some stuff together and Scott was confident enough in me to recommend me to one of his contacts.

Now here's the thing, as I was writing this, I hadn't been in touch with Scott any more than loosely on social media. We still like and trust each other, it's just that our lives have moved a little bit and we're both busy with stuff that doesn't involve the other.

That will change I'm sure, but in the meantime, I still have to continually make sure that I am refreshing my network by constantly meeting new people, either face to face or on social, and putting in the effort necessary to move those people closer to me.

People will drift in and out of your network for all sorts of reasons. It is most often nothing that you have done wrong or nothing that you could do anything about. Apart from our very close friends and family, very few people stay in the inner circle for a huge amount of time and it's natural for our relationships to ebb and flow.

The effort needs to be twofold. Constantly refreshing and bringing people into your network, while deepening each and every relationship.

The power of serendipity

I've been to so many networking events over the years and talked to so many people about the subject of networking that serendipity is a word that comes up very often.

The *Oxford English Dictionary* defines serendipity as "the occurrence and development of events by chance in a satisfactory or beneficial way, understanding the chance as any event that takes place in the absence of any obvious project".

In other words, serendipity is a happy accident, something that happens as a result of "being in the right place at the right time".

So many of my successes have been as a result of a serendipitous relationship, something that wasn't planned to be a big deal, such as commenting on someone's blog.

This is somewhere else where I have a conflict between working hard and working smart. People will often tell me that, in their opinion, it is only relevant to network if you are talking to the "right" people. One of the questions I am asked a lot is how to end a conversation if the person you're talking to isn't a "good" person to be talking to.

In my opinion, spending too much time strategizing over who you should and shouldn't speak to at networking events is time that would be better spent just talking to people.

Spending time agonizing over whether someone is the right person for you to be spending time with ignores the possibility for serendipity. What if that person, who you have just decided isn't worth you wasting your time on, is connected to the person you really should speak to?

Ah, you're wrong there, Stefan, I hear you say. Because actually, my business only sells stuff to accountants/pipe fitters/lap dancers (insert your particular niche here) and therefore I only want to speak to those people.

Or, as someone actually said to me after interrogating me for five minutes at a networking event, "I see, so you're *only* an employee/director? I only deal with the shareholder/directors. I should mingle with some other people."

He only deals with shareholder/directors. Like the ones who sat on the same board as me. Like the ones who asked my advice because I was the one "on the ground".

The person you're speaking to may well be your gateway to the people you really want to speak to. The person you're speaking to may well be perfect for you. Don't be so closed minded that you waste all your time strategizing, instead of actually talking to people.

Return on investment from networking and social media

If you look at any of my stories about my big successes, plus the other people around me who have made any sort of success from networking, we don't measure our return on investment from individual meetings or relationships.

In my relationship with Scott Torrance/Chris Marr, the financial return on investment was negative for me for at least the first year. For them too, I suspect.

We had put effort into building and nurturing the relationship, and none of us actually bought anything from the other. When the time was right, business took place.

Imagine if any one of us had given up. The crock of gold at the end of the rainbow would never have been found.

But that's what a lot of people do in networking, just as their contacts are getting close to the inner circle, just as people are developing the trust, just as they are finally breaking through, they stop, because it "wasn't working".

There are some easy wins, and by immersing yourself and putting in the right amount of effort, the process between which people meet you and when business takes place can be considerably shortened, but it does still need to be allowed to develop.

It is always the right time for you to sell, but everyone else has their own agenda, and it might not be the right time for them to buy yet.

Don't disappear just as people are reaching for their wallets.

Networking is a set of opportunities – not a magic sales dispensing machine. How you choose to use those opportunities, indeed whether you choose to use them at all, will have a huge impact on what results you get from your networking.

And networking is constant, it isn't just an event, it isn't just to be used when you need more sales. The adage that you should "build your network when you don't need it, so that it is there when you do" holds very true.

4
Finding the right networking events

So now you're ready. We've thought about networking, we've assembled our tools. Now it's time to find somewhere to start putting all of this into practice.

But where? Which networking events should you attend? Which networking event will suit you?

The type of networking event that suits you might, ironically, mean attending networking events that don't suit you at all.

I shall explain.

At some point in my career someone said to me "if you want to do business with accountants, find out where accountants go – and go there". The same principle pretty much applies here.

If you're using business networking to build your network for the sake of your business or career, then it is going to be more important to attend networking events that suit the people you want to meet rather than events that suit you.

The opportunities to network seem endless. As much as you can spend time making a strategy and researching which event will be best for you, there is much to be said for just getting stuck in, going to events, and starting to work out which are best for you.

Business networking events

You can easily find organized business networking events all over the place. Most towns will have several networking events, both formal and informal.

My experience has been that these sorts of networking events universally work if you approach them in the right way, which hopefully this book will help you to do.

If you want to find networking events in your own town, then a sensible place to start would be to Google "business networking YOURTOWN" and see what comes up.

There are also national organizations that organize events up and down the country.

4Networking – 4networking.biz

4Networking[1] runs over 5,000 networking events per year in England, Scotland, Wales and Australia.

---

[1] I am a long-time member of 4Networking and was formerly a director of 4Networking Ltd. I currently have no role or any financial interest in the organization.

One of the major benefits of 4Networking is that any member can attend any group, anywhere – something that certainly helped to speed up my reputation nationally, as well as locally and regionally.

BNI – bni.com

Business Networking International exists across the world now and describes itself as the "world's largest referral marketing organization". The organization is made of up local "chapters", primarily running early morning meetings specifically designed to get business owners passing referrals to each other.

Chambers of Trade and Commerce

UK – http://www.britishchambers.org.uk/
US – https://www.uschamber.com/
Australia – https://www.acci.asn.au/

Chambers of Trade and Commerce exist to promote the interests of their local business members. Certainly in the UK that often involves organizing networking meetings and bringing local businesses together.

Chamber events do very often include businesses that aren't regularly found at other networking events, such as independent local retailers.

To find a local networking event, you will need to find your local chamber first and then make contact to see what networking events they hold.

The Federation of Small Businesses (FSB) – http://www.fsb.org.uk/

In the UK the FSB exists as a business support and lobbying group for the interests of its small business members.

They do organize networking events, and again you would need to contact the local representative to find out exactly what that means in your area.

The Institute of Directors – http://www.iod.com/

Describing themselves as "the UK's longest running organization for professional leaders" the IOD provide professional development and training for business owners in the UK.

They also organize networking events across the UK; once again, these are organized by the local office.

Rotary Club International – https://www.rotary.org/

Arguably the world's first formalized networking organization, Rotary now exists internationally. They are no longer specifically a networking organization, as their stated remit is much more about supporting communities. Nevertheless, their structure ensures that members do form strong connections with their fellow members.

Trade and business events and conferences

The opportunities to network with people in the same or a related industry or profession are so often overlooked.

Whatever your business or career it is likely you get invited to all sorts of events, seminars and conferences every year.

If you're not currently getting invited, get onto Google (other search engines do exist, or so I'm told) and look for events you can get to and meet other people.

Very often, for the professions particularly, these events will offer so many hours of continuing professional development, plus you get the chance to network with your peers, including, potentially, those who may have an opportunity for you in the future, particularly if you keep in touch.

Networking at trade shows, business shows and conferences

Another great opportunity to network exists at the trade shows, business shows and conferences you will attend in the normal course of your business.

If you're a small business owner in the UK you have plenty of opportunities to network at shows like these.

These shows tend to have hundreds, if not thousands, of attendees. The potential to start conversations with people, and bring them into your crowd, is huge, and plenty of people never take advantage of it.

Make sure that you treat any shows such as these as the start of the conversation. The return on investment should not be measured in what sales you get on the day, but what opportunities you create to build relationships.

Some shows in the UK that are well worth checking out are:

National shows

The Business Show – London –
http://www.thebusinessshow.co.uk/

The Business Show, incorporating The Business StartUp Show, runs two large events in London each year. In the spring they have an event at ExCeL in East London and in the autumn you will find them at Olympia.

This is a show on a grand scale, with around 25,000 attendees over two days and massive opportunities to network, listen to inspiring speakers and visit the hundreds of exhibitors.

The Business Networking Show –
http://thebusinessnetworkingshow.info/

A once-a-year show dedicated to all things networking, with attendees from all the UK's major business networking organizations.

Held in September in Wolverhampton, the show attracts around 1,000 attendees from all over the UK. As you would expect from the name of the show, the opportunities to network during the day are immense. There are plenty of speakers, picked from leading entrepreneurs in the UK, as well as up and coming speakers, all of whom have a useful and unique message.

The Welsh Business Shows –
http://thewelshbusinessshows.co.uk/

There are two shows per year, one in the spring in Cardiff and one in the autumn in Swansea promoting entrepreneurial Wales.

These shows have a very busy vibe, with lots going on throughout the day and a mixture of speakers picked from the business world in Wales, plus speakers brought in from other parts of the UK.

Expo Scotland – http://www.exposcotland.co.uk/

Once a year in Glasgow, Expo Scotland brings together Scottish-based exhibitors, attendees and speakers to promote not just business in Scotland, but to promote Scottish businesses to the rest of the UK.

Regional shows

Around the UK are many regional shows that are well worth visiting. Typically free to attend, the shows offer a great opportunity to meet a lot of local business people, in one day. These shows try very hard to bring great speakers to their region too.

Exposure Events – http://www.exposure-events.com/

Based in the North East, Exposure run shows in various regions in England and Scotland.

Memo Events – http://www.memoevents.co.uk/

Based in the South of England, Memo have flagship events across the south including the Southampton Business Show and Portsmouth Expo.

Thames Valley Expo – http://www.thamesvalleyexpo.co.uk/

Based, as you would guess, in the Thames Valley, these shows, typically in Windsor and Swindon, have a great reputation as busy shows, with keynote speakers from around the UK.

Kent B2B – http://www.kentb2b.co.uk/

Kent B2B provide very well-attended shows across Kent, typically sponsored by the Chamber of Commerce.

The Business Growth Show – http://thebusinessgrowthshow.com/

Midlands-based, The Business Growth Show have been around for over ten years now and organize well-attended and supported shows with speakers from around the UK.

At any of these shows, you will meet people you don't normally meet at networking events. There are usually organized networking events throughout the day.

To me, one of the great reasons for attending is that you immediately have something in common with everyone else in the room – you're all at the same show. Remembering my advice from earlier, about going for the "lowest common denominator", means that you can start a conversation with anyone there.

And, as ever, the potential is that most people won't bother. Most people will decide they have something better to do that day, but if you are there, you have the chance to be in the right place at the right time.

You don't have to go to networking events to network

You are constantly presented with situations where you can expand and/or deepen your network.

This does *not* involve thrusting your business card at every new contact you meet though, in the hope they will want to buy from you (you know that guy, don't be that guy).

Striking up conversations with people, particularly when you already have something in common (which you *always* do, more of that later), can lead to opportunities, whether those opportunities are business related or simply the chance for you to have a new and interesting person in your network.

I always think Jameson's Irish Whiskey sums this up best: "there is no such thing as **strangers**, only **friends** we haven't met yet".

5
Making networking events work for you

I think it's easy to get sucked into the idea that you just need to turn up to networking meetings and events in order for them to work for you.

I also think that making some changes to how you approach networking meetings can make a huge difference to your success from those meetings.

The structure of meetings run by organizations such as 4Networking and BNI and the lack of structure of open networking meetings both have huge opportunities. They also offer a lot of missed opportunities where people choose to be either lulled into a false sense of security by the structure or refuse to get out of their comfort zones.

The real magic and the real opportunity in networking meetings is in working that little bit harder than anyone else in the room to form connections and then work with those connections to deepen the relationship.

Expand your opportunity by being there longer

This is a really simple one. At every networking event I have been to, there is a period of open networking before the formal part of the meeting starts.

Be the first there. Don't lie in and pitch up late. Don't sit in the car park and catch up on emails. Get into the meeting and start connecting with people.

I used to abhor the open networking bit at the beginning of meetings and would have a plan to arrive just before the formal part of the meeting started. It took me *far* too long to realize how many opportunities I was missing.

By arriving at the meeting early you can start more conversations with more people and, if there are people you particularly want to talk to, you are more likely to get to them before other people do.

Mini one to one meetings

If you *really* want to have a conversation with someone who you know is attending the same networking meeting as you, connect with them on social media beforehand and ask outright if you can have a one to one with them at the meeting. Or use the time before meetings to have mini one to one meetings with people. Either way, get to know them a little bit better before the formal part of the meeting starts and, if you think there is more of a conversation to be had, ask them for a one to one either during the meeting, if the meeting format allows it, or after the meeting.

Maximize the use of your networking time before the meeting, then you can concentrate on what needs to be done in the formal part of the meeting.

Shamelessly self-promote using whatever means are made available to you

If you have the opportunity to display promotional material during the event, make sure you do.

- Some events have a bumf table to display your leaflets and brochures.
- If at all possible, take a banner stand.

These will be on display throughout the meeting and will constantly remind people of what you do. After people have had conversations with you, they will be able to browse your leaflet and look at your banner. After your 40 or 60 seconds the banner will act as a subtle reminder, reinforcing your message.

It is often said in marketing that it takes more than one "touch" for your prospects to get your message, that you need to deliver the message in as many different ways as possible. Displaying your material as well as having conversations with people and presenting your 40 or 60 seconds simply takes full advantage of the two or three hours you will be at the meeting to further reinforce your marketing message.

Starting conversations – going for the lowest common denominator

One of the questions I am asked constantly is how to start conversations in the open networking part of meetings.

I used to wonder the same and used to believe the blogs and articles I read which suggested that there were some "power phrases" or clever approaches I could use that would guarantee success.

The trouble with using a scripted approach is that the other guy might not have the same script as you.

So I learned to go for the lowest common denominator, by finding something I definitely, undoubtedly had in common with the other person and starting the conversation on that basis.

For a start, you're at the same networking meeting. A very simple "hi, have you been to this meeting before" works.

Once I spotted someone I **really** wanted to talk to, they were the person responsible for booking speakers and trainers in a BIG and well known organization. It was the end of a conference and we were both involved in breaking down our respective stands. I went in with the opener "breaking down stands hey – what a *pita*!". He laughed, we got into conversation and it turned into a massive opportunity for me.

There is so much you have in common with others in the room:

You've driven through the same traffic.
The weather (I'm English, it's our national sport).
You're watching the same presentation or seminar.
You're looking for the tea or coffee.

The key here is that everyone else in the room is human too. There is no need to think about overly clever ways of opening conversations, just because it's a networking meeting.

Demonstrating your personal brand

Remember that during any networking meeting you are on show. As much as I implore you not to judge or underestimate anyone else in the room, they are making judgements about what you do.

If you want people to believe you are a certain type of business person, you need to be living that throughout the meeting.

I've seen the disorganized personal assistant. I've seen the presentation skills trainer who couldn't string his own words together. I've seen the confidence coach who hid in the corner for most of the meeting.

When you arrive, when you talk to people, when you present your 40 or 60 seconds, make sure you are presenting yourself in the way you want people to think about you.

Through the room or to the room?

I've often been told that networking is about selling through the room rather than to the room; that the real opportunity lies in who the people in the room know rather than just the people in the room themselves.

I don't think that the two things are exclusive. I believe that it is your responsibility though to make it as clear as possible what you do and, if you are in an environment where you are inviting referrals, to make it as clear as possible who you are looking to speak to.

Think about packaging what you do in soundbites that people can easily take away and that will help them remember exactly what it is you do. This isn't about a memorable tagline at the end of your 60 seconds. This is about being specific, in one sentence, about the real benefit you bring to the people you do business with.

It's your job to make it simple for people to understand what you do. Talk to people around you and ask for honest feedback. Is your introduction making it crystal clear what services you offer? Do people completely "get" the benefit of paying you?

For a lot of people offering consultancy or training (me included), if I explained to people exactly what I do, their eyes would glaze over and I would never make a sale. People are interested in the benefit of what you do. Will paying you £1 return them £1.20 in terms of better sales, more profit, savings on something? If so, make sure that is crystal clear and, as explained in Chapter 3, use real-life testimonials to bring that to life.

Own your 40 seconds

No matter whether you feel confident about delivering your 40 or 60 seconds or not, there are some simple ways to completely own the space and get people paying attention to you, and wanting to have a one to one meeting with you to find out more.

You must prepare for this.

This is your opportunity to engage with the people in the room and it is far too important to leave to chance.

- Stand up and breathe.
- Stand away from the chair and do not lean on it.
- Stand firmly on both legs, don't cross them.
- Don't cross your arms.
- Follow the structure from Chapter 2 – Putting together your networking toolkit.
- Try to make eye contact with people in the room, specifically people you would like to talk to.
- Be clear about your call to action – tell people what they need to do next to take the relationship forward.
- Breathe, smile and sit down.

But practise this over and over again. I maintain that the 40 or 60-second round isn't as important as the follow-up and everything else that we do in networking; but it is still important and is still a huge opportunity to make an impact.

NB. This is a business meeting. Unless you are a professional comedian do *not* try to be amusing or insert a joke. I have seen this go wrong far more times than I have seen it go right. It simply isn't worth the risk.

Make time to accept one to one requests from anyone and everyone who asks

In any other environment outside networking, if you delivered a sales message, in 40 seconds, that was so powerful that you had people queuing up to find out more, you would talk to everyone right?

I see people at networking meetings turning people away who may be genuinely interested in their services, often because they have already booked their three one to ones or, bizarrely, because they haven't left time at the end of the meeting to have extra one to ones.

You may never see these people again. They may have been so turned on by your message that they are dying to find out more. However, because you only allowed until 10am, they now don't get the chance to find out more, you don't get the chance to tell them more about you and, because they have a busy life too, they will forget what they were so turned on about almost as soon as they leave the meeting.

Aim to allow at least half an hour after the official end time of the networking meeting in case anyone else wants to find out more about you or you need to extend your one to one with someone particularly promising.

If you are going to be spending time at the networking meeting, then spending an extra half hour before the meeting and an extra half hour at the end of the meeting, and spending that time having actual conversations with people, will make a significant difference to your success from the event.

Your one to ones are sales meetings not sales broadcasts

Your 40 seconds was your opportunity to broadcast your message. You had an attentive audience (sure, some of them were tweeting/replying to emails/checking their bank balance but that's just life in 2016) and it was the right time during the meeting to broadcast.

Your one to ones are not a broadcast. These are now your opportunity to further develop the relationship and, to use a very salesy word, qualify the person you are talking to.

Ask plenty of questions about the other person's business. If you solve a particular problem, then try to ask questions that establish whether the person you are talking to has that problem.

Find out as much as you can about them and their business and *don't* try to promote your business here.

This is where I believe most people go wrong, by trying too hard to stuff what they do into a ten-minute conversation in a busy meeting.

If you were to cold call someone, the point of the call would not be to try to sell to them immediately. The point of the call would be to qualify whether they needed or wanted what you had to sell, and then try to organize another appointment to discuss it with them further, outside of the pressure of the cold call.

Your one to ones can be exactly the same. Talk to the other person and if, and only if, you genuinely think that what you offer will be of use, then ask for another appointment. Almost everyone carries a diary with them these days, typically on their smartphone. Even if they don't, ask for permission to call the next day to set up an appointment.

Strike while the iron is hot and, most importantly, be proactive and take control of the conversation. Someone said to me recently "oh, I just tell people what I do. If they need me I'm sure they will come back to me."

No they won't. What they will do is forget who you are. Or lose your business card. Or come across someone else who does something similar and who is more proactive and use their services instead.

When opportunities present themselves, it is up to you to take them forward. Most small business owners don't, and that's where the opportunity lies for people like you, who will.

Building your reputation as a public speaker and an authority on your subject

Many networking events give their members the opportunity to speak in front of the other members, usually for around 10/15 minutes. Both 4Networking and BNI have a member presentation (a 4Sight in 4N's terminology, the ten-minute speaker slot in BNIs) as part of their standard meeting format.

The chance here to build your profile both as an authority on your subject and as a public speaker is just enormous, and, once again, a chance that very few people take full advantage of.

If you take the 4Networking structure, where any member can speak at any of the meetings anywhere in the UK, the potential for accelerating your national profile and building your network rapidly is astonishing.

Think about this: everyone claims to be brilliant at what they do, but a person who puts themselves out of their comfort zone and is prepared to talk about their subject in front of an audience of their peers is seen as an authority on that subject.

When I wanted people to start to consider me a thought leader on networking, one of the things that I immediately did was to start talking about it in front of any audience anywhere.

A mistake that a lot of people make is to wait until they feel they are confident enough to be a public speaker before they ever start.

The mistake here is that nobody is ever confident before they start doing something. The way to get confident is to do it and, I'm sorry to break it to you, do it badly for a while.

If you haven't yet read Susan Jeffers' excellent book *Feel the Fear and Do It Anyway* I strongly recommend that you do. She sums all of this up far better than I have scope to do in this book.

Suffice to say, my first attempts at delivering the speaker slot at networking meetings were pretty much me reading out loud while hiding behind the sheet of A4 paper I had my presentation written on. I would stop about every 30 seconds for a sip of water and I dried up or had a minor panic attack many times. But I did it, pushed through my nerves and now have a reputation as a popular (and confident) speaker.

There are some ways in which you can easily feel more prepared for your first speaking slot at a networking event.

First, prepare. It sounds stupid, but in the same way that a lot of people don't prepare for their 40-second introduction, I spot a lot of people not preparing for their 4Sight or ten-minute slot.

Think about your headline message. What do you want people to come away with? This should not even be an attempt at a sales pitch, but an opportunity to demonstrate that you really know your stuff, as well as giving people an idea of just how passionate you are about your work.

What knowledge do you have that would be of massive benefit to your audience? What could they take away and use right now?

What insights do you have into life or business that would be of interest to a proportion of your audience? What have you done as part of your work or personal life that would make people in your audience sit up and think "wow".

What could you tell people in your audience that might mean that some of them have something in common with you? What can you give people that helps to make you memorable? Maybe you share a hobby or interest that will resonate with some people in the audience? Maybe you have achieved some challenge that other people will have been thinking about doing but didn't know how to organize?

Maybe you have overcome a personal or business challenge and the insight into how you overcame it you believe will be powerful and helpful to other people there.

Perhaps you learned something in your previous life or career that, although apparently unrelated to your current business, gave you lessons or discipline that has proven invaluable to you, and may do so to your audience.

Prepare what you're going to say and work out how you will deliver it. Write the presentation and deliver it to yourself in a mirror more than once. Or to your family (who will laugh, get used to it) or to your cat (who won't laugh but may get bored and wander off).

Second, get out there and practise. Your networking group and the people at the group are likely to want to support you as you embark on your first presentations. I have never, in over 1,000 meetings, seen any speaker encounter negative or hostile feedback from their networking peers. Quite the opposite, I have seen people supported, applauded and, in my case, in the early days of my speaking to networking audiences I got so much valuable feedback, which I am still remembering and putting into practice to this day.

I would recommend presenting a few times locally, getting feedback from your local members and tweaking and improving your presentation so that it feels right for you and you start to deliver it with a little more confidence.

Then get busy and get it out there to as wide an audience as you choose.

If you're a 4Networking member, all you need to do is track down the details of the group leader or area leader at the meetings you want to present to, call them and ask them to book you into their next available slot.

If you're a member of a different networking organization, then work out how to get speaking slots at other groups and start to book it and get out there.

If you have a local trade show or expo, then they are likely to be looking for speakers. Here's a hint. They will often favour paid exhibitors as speakers at their events. If you decide to book a stand, you may be in with a better chance of being a speaker there and doing so before you're well known as a speaker.

In 2010 I did exactly this and set off on a road trip, presenting my 4Sight to networking groups all over the UK. In one week I did Weston Super Mare, Harrogate, Durham and Edinburgh. I also took myself all over England, Scotland and Wales.

Instantly, people's perception was that I was worth listening to because I had travelled so far to see them. My natural inclination is to try to deliver massive value to people who take the time to turn up for me, so they would walk away talking about my presentation; and, within a few short months, I had a reputation as being someone who knew his stuff about networking, and that reputation spread throughout the UK.

That early tour undoubtedly led to some of the huge opportunities I have subsequently been fortunate enough to be offered. I've watched other people around me emulate that process too, with similar results.

What is really important is that most people won't bother. So if you do, you instantly give yourself a higher profile than those who don't.

Whenever and wherever you speak, make sure you leave with collateral and with people to follow up with.

By collateral I mean photos of you talking in front of different sized audiences. If you've got your phone with you (and I can't imagine you wouldn't), then ask someone in the audience to take a few snaps.

This is vital. Make sure you share those photos on social media – "here I am speaking this morning to a networking group in sometown". You are speaking not just to the audience in the room but to your social contacts who will start to notice your profile building as well.

If someone wants to Periscope, or otherwise video your presentation, let them, it's a great way to expose your material and presentation to a wider audience.

Building your profile as an authority on your subject by speaking about it is another instant way to speed up your results from networking.

Attend meetings with positive intent

Expect to receive something positive at each and every networking meeting you attend.

I've come across so many people who seem to decide that networking isn't going to work for them and then, perversely, spend time and effort proving that's the case.

The return on investment from networking meetings isn't measured in immediate sales. A lot of these connections you are making will take your time and your effort to move forward, just as any other relationship in a sales environment would.

At the end of each and every networking meeting make notes and schedule yourself reminders about what happened. Who you talked to. What promises were made to follow up.

And then keep your first promise to people and do so.

Your attitude towards the events you attend will make a difference to your results. But your attitude, more importantly, will lead to changes in how you approach the events you attend, and that will make an even bigger difference.

Turning up and hoping that something positive will happen is one thing. Turning up, hoping that something positive will happen *and* taking the actions necessary to make it happen is what will really make the instant difference.

6
Following up

I am potentially about to save you a great deal of time.

If you're not going to follow up on your networking relationships you can stop networking now.

Genuinely, stay in bed. Have another cup of tea. Don't ever go networking again because you are seriously wasting your time.

In fact, you can even stop reading this book now, because the rest of it will not do you any good.

Let me tell you some things that happen to you as you leave a networking event:

- You have a missed call from a client.
- You have a text from your 15-year-old son's school asking why he is absent today (or is that just me?).
- You have an email that needs to be dealt with urgently.
- You have another meeting in 15 minutes and you're 20 minutes' drive away and have only 10 minutes' worth of petrol.

And so the little conversations you have had at the networking event, the mini one to ones, other people's

40-second introduction, even the full-length one to one meetings, all of that slips way down your priority list in favour of getting to your next appointment while simultaneously trying to reply to an email *and* find out why the hell your son didn't get out of bed.

Someone told me recently that they don't follow up because "I've told people what I do. They'll remember and get in touch if they need me."

No.

They won't.

Life will get in the way and they will vaguely remember meeting you, but have no idea what they did with your contact details.

Because everyone else's life is just the same as ours and yet, knowing how busy and distracted we are, we put a different set of rules onto everyone else and expect them to remember us despite everything else that is going on in their life.

Most people don't ever bother to follow up after networking events. So the massive opportunity exists for those of us who do, and particularly for those of us who do it brilliantly.

It is our job and our responsibility to remind people that we exist, not theirs to keep remembering us.

That's the end of my rant. Presuming you're still reading, I'm going to have a look at some ways you can follow up.

We talked about having your CRM set up and ready a few chapters ago. You have done that, haven't you? You have at the very least set up some sort of system to record people and conversations? If not, please do. Stop now and do so. It will make you so much more successful if you put a simple workable system in place.

The first step in following up is to record every conversation and every meaningful interaction.

Ideally at the end of every networking meeting, before you leave, record the details of the people you had conversations with and, crucially, record any action points from those conversations.

Action points might be:

- You promised to phone to arrange another one to one
- You offered to email them details of a contact who might be useful to them
- They asked for copies of your free ebook
- You suggested another networking event they might like to attend and said you would send details
- They expressed interest in what you do.

Even if there was no explicit action point, I strongly suggest you make an action point to follow up with them.

When registering people I have met on my CRM, I also go to some extra effort.

First, I search for all of their social media profiles, specifically Twitter, LinkedIn and Facebook, and make sure I have recorded them as well. Capsule actually includes your contacts' social feed in their activity on their record, which I find particularly helpful. It also uses their profile photo from either Twitter or LinkedIn if you add that to their record. I also, of course, connect with them on whichever platforms they are active on.

Second, I go to their website and use that to record such things as their address and any other contact information that may be on there.

Lastly, I look out for any blog posts or articles they have recently written and make sure I read them and, if appropriate, like, comment and/or share them.

NOTE: I actually use Evernote to scan people's business cards in with my iPhone. This reads their contact details directly into my Contacts, with astonishing accuracy, and, simultaneously, finds them on LinkedIn and offers to connect with them.

From there, I use the Import from the Contacts function in Capsule to drop them straight into my CRM.

I'm a massive fan of technology when it works and, in this case, it certainly does.

Active and passive following up

If someone expresses interest in what you do or, during a conversation you explicitly agreed some sort of action, then you will be actively following up with them.

Active follow-up is when that follow-up relates to a specific conversation or stated need. For example, if someone wants to have a second conversation with you, or for you to send them something. Then your follow-up is active.

Passive follow-up, on the other hand, is just as relevant, and more difficult to pin down. This is the act of keeping in touch with people, just to remind them that you're there, until the opportunity comes to move into a more active relationship.

For active follow-up, you will use direct methods, such as phone and email. For passive follow-up, you can make full use of social media and content marketing.

First, and most importantly, if you have told someone you will follow up, do so, and get that next appointment booked. The phone is definitely the best way to do so.

Remember that because you have met at a networking event this is *not* a cold call. You talked, you promised to follow up and now you're doing so. This, for me, is one of the major benefits of networking – I never have to cold call again!

If you have promised or offered to provide some information, then email is the best bet. Do it promptly, as quickly as you can after the event and schedule a time to call to follow up after that.

I also follow up with people by postcard, particularly if I just want to thank them for spending time with me, and commenting on their website, or LinkedIn profile, or whatever impressed me.

Once again, I use technology for this and use an app called Touchnote on my iPhone. Touchnote allows me to use my own photographs to create a postcard, add the recipient's address and a message and send it direct from my phone. It arrives two or three days later and costs about £1 per card. If I have taken a selfie with the person I'm sending it to, I will use that as the image, and, if not, will use one of my quotes or an appropriate picture. My experience is that people *really* appreciate this and tend to keep the postcards.

PS: I also use Touchnote to send cards to my clients. You can use it to send postcards all over the world for the same £1 per card. (I also use it to keep my grandmother up to date with where in the world I happen to be that week.)

For most businesses, some sort of formal or semi-formal follow-up process would help.

When I first started my business I found that I was "reinventing the wheel" with every contact. Every time I spoke to someone new I relied on memory, with no system at all to make sure I followed up.

Now, using my CRM, I put each contact or enquiry into what Capsule calls a "Track" (every CRM will have something similar). That then sets tasks and reminders at certain times, either after another event or at a fixed point. So, for example, I have a reminder to call people after 24 hours, then to send an email immediately, then to call again after seven days.

I have different "tracks" based on the type of enquiry, so someone who enquires about my speaking at an event will be put into a different track to someone who I met at a networking event and enquires about one to one coaching. Rather than trying to remember when to call someone, these days I get a reminder on my phone. Rather than rewriting every single email, certain things such as my fees for speaking are templated.

NOTE: It is vital to respond to enquiries and follow up personally rather than just with a copy and pasted template. I *always* send a unique response, then with the standard information templated.

Remember every time that not only is it ok to follow up, it's vital.

Passive following up is achieved by being around the people who might, in the future, be interested in what you do and ensuring that you are constantly reminding them of your existence. Business networking offers a huge opportunity to do this because you can make sure that you are always visible to the people around you, in a meaningful way.

If you're attending networking meetings, so that people can see that you are still doing what you do, and they can see that other people are doing business with you, then it will constantly and subtly remind them of your services.

Other people talking about doing business with you as well is, of course, a fantastic form of advertising, because the person who might not have been convinced first time round is much more likely to listen to their peers.

A few times recently I've attended a networking event and someone has said to me "I'm really pleased you're here, I've been meaning to call you…" before telling me how they're really interested in working with me or attending The Networking Retreat.

On each occasion, it turns out they've been "meaning to phone" me for weeks, if not months. It's just that it wasn't at the top of their list of priorities and they hadn't got round to it. My being at the event reminded them that they wanted to speak to me, and so they did.

One of the huge benefits of business networking and social media is that it gives you the opportunity to be there, to remind people that you exist, and to prompt people who've been "meaning to phone" you and simply haven't got round to it.

Everyone has their own stuff going on. They might really want to buy from us, but it isn't urgent and, just as with our own lives, the urgent stuff gets in the way. Stuff like making a living, helping the kids with their homework, being #dadtaxi, or whatever it is that takes up your time.

Being there consistently, both in the real world and in people's timelines online, reminds them that we are there and gives them the opportunity to speak to us easily, without making yet another phone call, which they might not have time to do.

How many people have been "meaning to call" you and haven't got round to it? And how easy have you made it for them?

Remember, it's your job to remind people that you exist and to make it easy for them to buy from you.

Be there at networking events and online and give people easy opportunities to follow up with you and to buy from you if they're intending to.

Of course, the more people see you, the more your message is being reinforced, the more the Meet–Like–Know–Trust is moving forward.

Your silent audience

One of the things that I have really noticed recently is that, in 2016, your network and your audience may well be bigger than you think, and you might not even know how close some of that network is to you.

I've been to a couple of networking events recently where people who I thought were right on the outskirts of my network have asked for a one to one with me and subsequently booked onto The Networking Retreat. These aren't people I talk to regularly, they're not on my Business Networking Not For Dummies mailing list, and I had no idea they were interested in what I was putting out there. Put simply, I had no idea they might be interested in buying from me. But in the background, they had been reading my blogs, watching my videos and making a note to talk to me when they next had the opportunity.

It used to be simple; you would have a business card holder and your network existed in there. Latterly, you had an email mailing list and you knew exactly how many people were on it; they were the people you were engaging with.

But now a lot of your audience may be silent. They may have met you at a networking event or connected with you somewhere on social media and that may have been the very last contact you had, or so you thought. They might not even have ever met you or connected with you, but are still looking at what you put out there.

The people who use some of their time to like, comment on or share your stuff are visible. You probably (and if you don't you should) take the time to thank them and engage with them on their turf too. But there is also the silent army of people who might be reading your content, or watching your videos, or watching your tweets, and never commenting, liking or sharing.

This is why passive follow-up is *so* important today. Active follow-up is where you know who the person is, they've expressed an interest in doing business with you and you follow up accordingly.

Passive follow-up is where you put engaging content out there and then regularly remind people that you have products or services they might want to buy. Passive follow-up is where you continue to engage, even with those people in your network who aren't responding and are silent.

I know it sounds a little 1984, but in the 21st century you really don't know who is watching you. The question is:

are you giving them something to watch? Because if you're not, someone else who does the same as you probably is.

Asking for the order

There comes a point in every business relationship where one person is going to buy from the other one, when someone has to ask for the order.

And this is an area which I genuinely think scares a lot of people who go networking.

Let's start with a realistic assumption. People who go to business networking events are business people. Business people accept that as much as they need to sell, they also occasionally need to buy. And if a service is going to be valuable to them, they will want to buy it.

Make it easy for people to buy from you

Recently, I met a lady at a networking event. She did follow up with me by email the next day and her email read along the lines of: "lovely to meet you, I think what I do would be great for your business, when can you next come to <A TOWN QUITE A LONG WAY AWAY> so we can have coffee and I can tell you about it?"

First, 10/10 for even following up. You know it's a bugbear of mine that far too many people don't follow up after networking events.

But if you want to sell to me, why are you expecting me to come to you? Why not suggest that you come to me. Come to that, it's 2015, the telephone has been invented and so have Skype, FaceTime, webinars and Google Hangouts. Now we've met we could very easily have had a conversation that didn't involve either of us travelling.

There are so many examples of people putting all the legwork into networking and building an audience, and then putting obstacles in the way of people ever buying from them.

Think about what you do. Are you making it easy for people to buy from you? Or are you setting anyone who shows an interest a virtual obstacle course before they part with any money?

Here's another, personal example. People often ask if they can buy my book at networking events, and in the past, if they didn't have a tenner on them at that moment, my only other option was to send them an Amazon link. Nowadays I carry a credit card terminal with me. If people are in the mood to buy, I make it easy for them to do so there and then, before the moment passes and they get distracted by something else. Result? I now sell 50% more books at networking events than I used to.

Instead of building obstacles, build shortcuts. Let people get to you and your services as simply and quickly as possible.

The final ask

It has been said that the main reason why people don't buy is that nobody asks for the order. Most of the time, believe it or not, people need reassurance and direction in where to go next.

If you know that what you are selling is perfect for the person you are talking to, if you have answered their questions and built the relationship sufficiently, if you've done your groundwork, then take a deep breath and say:

"Shall we go ahead then?"

That one question, applied often enough, will have a massive impact on your networking success if you have done everything else to build and nurture the relationship.

Work out a way of asking for the order that works for you. And go for it.

I have spent so much time talking about following up simply because this is where it is possible to make such a big difference to your results from networking.

If you are getting your networking meetings "right" and delivering a passionate introduction, having mini one to ones and positive conversations with the other attendees, then your follow-up may well be the final touch needed to convert those conversations into sales.

Even if you feel you aren't smashing the events themselves yet, the follow-up is where you have the opportunity to continue those relationships and conversations in an environment that you feel much more comfortable with. So many people have said to me that they don't ever feel completely confident when talking to a room full of people, but are brilliant when talking one to one. If you've taken the trouble to get out of your comfort zone and attend networking events, you owe it to yourself to allow yourself to shine, and follow up with the people you could talk to one to one.

And I haven't even really started on using social media yet!

7
How to instantly win on social media

Social media, in my opinion, brought about the biggest change in how we manage our personal and business relationships since the telephone was invented.

Social is such a young form of communication, and still so widely misunderstood, that the opportunity for those who do choose to integrate it as part of their overall networking strategy is beyond huge.

Furthermore, the opportunity for those who are prepared to put really massive effort into their social and online presence is overwhelming.

If you're reading this in 2016 and still believe you can get by in business without fully adopting social media, then you are mistaken. When people are looking for products or services they want or need, they are turning to Google and to their friends online.

And even more than that, if a trusted friend is talking about a product or service online, then people are significantly more likely to check out that product or service.

The conversation is happening. People are talking about your products or services, or at the very least they are talking about products or services similar to yours. And they're talking about them on Twitter, Facebook, LinkedIn, Instagram, Periscope, YouTube, WhatsApp, Snapchat, Pinterest and on the thousands of other social platforms that now exist.

This chapter isn't about where you start with social; it's about how you can dominate on social.

Joining up networking and social media means that you always have a chance to add people to your network. You can be, almost, constantly engaging with new people and getting to know them.

Joining up networking and social media means that you always have a chance to deepen those relationships and bring value to the relationships, before you ever need to "sell".

I'm going to focus specifically in this chapter on how you can use several social channels to achieve this and will be looking at Twitter, Instagram, Facebook, Facebook pages, YouTube and Periscope. (These aren't in order of preference, simply the order in which I typed them. I also acknowledge that there are many other platforms, it is simply that these are the ones that, at the time of writing, seem to be the most important, and most popular, among networkers.)

And, before you start, I haven't forgotten LinkedIn. In fact LinkedIn is *so* important it warrants a chapter all to itself.

Overall though, and thinking outside the labels for the different social platforms, these are simply new methods for talking to each other. Many methods have been invented over time – printed books, radio, telephone, television, email and the internet and at every stage people have worked out how to use them and, of course, businesses have then tried to work out how to take advantage of the new technology.

There are still some doubters, of course, who believe that social is a fad. It isn't. It's here to stay. Look at how 15-year-olds are immersed in social. In ten years' time they are the people we will be doing business with. Social isn't just here to stay, social is here as an integral part of day-to-day life. Social is bigger than television and radio. Social isn't just a two-way conversation, but it is 24/7.

One of the biggest lessons I have learnt along the way with social media is that first you have to get onto the other person's turf. Before ever broadcasting your stuff, make sure that you have engaged with them and shown genuine and real interest in their stuff. I have won more friends and more business on social by liking, sharing and commenting on other people's tweets and posts than I have done by broadcasting my own.

People read my content, because I demonstrably read theirs.

Embrace social, and use it as an integral part of your overall communications.

People often ask me how much time I spend on social media. And it's a really difficult question to answer. I currently use an iPhone 6 Plus and to all intents and purposes I am "on" social media all the time I'm not driving, sleeping or engaging in something else that requires my full attention.

While travelling, during the evenings, while walking, while doing most things; I also have notifications set on my phone and on my smart watch, which will alert me if I have anyone engaging with me anywhere on social. And I make a point of trying to answer every single engagement, personally.

This isn't about whether I'm spending too much time on social though, this is about social being a vital place for me to spend my time. There are more people who are likely to buy one of my books or book me as a speaker on social at any one time than there are in my house watching TV. So I choose to talk to people on social media constantly and personally.

You never know where that huge opportunity is hiding, and that person, that contact who may lead you to your next biggest opportunity, may be the same person who just favourited, liked, shared, retweeted or otherwise engaged with you somewhere on social. So to me it makes absolute commercial sense to return the favour and engage with them.

Let's look at each platform and how you might use each one to move your network forward instantly.

Twitter

I started using Twitter in July 2008 and it stands the test of time as a simple way to maintain a conversation at scale, as well being able to have more personal conversations, almost one to one.

Twitter continues to innovate and add functionality to the platform, some of which I have taken huge advantage of, but the basic principle remains the same – Twitter is a conversation that is happening right now, whether or not you are taking part. Twitter is the fastest moving of the social platforms, which is why sometimes people struggle to get to grips with it, and where it has huge advantage for those who do learn how to use it.

If you want to instantly score on Twitter, then start interacting with a passion. Learn about the people you are following. Read what they're tweeting, take notice of their profile and engage with them on their terms.

Get stuck into their conversations and, if they tweet something of interest, reply, quote and/or retweet.

One of the most recent innovations from Twitter is the ability to reply with a short video tweet. I'm using this, particularly when new people follow or engage with me after I have spoken at an event.

To use Twitter video replies, in the native Twitter app on Android or iOS, when you either reply or compose a new tweet, you will see a camera icon bottom left. Click on that icon, then click the video camera icon, once again bottom left. Finally, click the icon that enables the front camera, point it at your face and start recording.

I have found that people really appreciate the tiny extra effort that goes into video replies (they're only 20ish seconds long maximum; this isn't something you will spend hours doing). What people have told me is that it has helped them feel like they "know" me much quicker, which has certainly led to people coming to my seminars and events, and has led to book sales.

Getting involved in hashtags is enormously valuable on Twitter. If you have been to an event, it is likely that that event has a hashtag. For example, The Business Networking Show in 2016 will have the hashtag #tbns2016. On Twitter this hashtag is searchable. It means that you are able to find people with whom you already have something in common – they have been to the same event as you or are following a story or interest that you share as well. I'm writing this during the Rugby World Cup and am avidly following and commenting on the conversations that are taking place around that. I'm also a Star Wars fan and, in October 2015 as I write, I am keeping an eye on the "#chewiewerehome" hashtag to find out news about the upcoming film.

In your profession or industry there will be hashtags that are also relevant to you in a business sense, as well as the social stuff, which glues the relationships together.

Instagram

As well as giving you the chance to engage and reply to other people's posts on Instagram, the potential to create easily shareable content on Instagram is huge.

Short (16-second) videos and attractive images are the mainstay of Instagram. The beauty of Instagram is that everything is so easily and quickly digestible and shareable.

Personal videos of the user talking briefly to camera or engaged in some relevant activity appear to get great traction and engagement on Instagram. The art of getting your message into 16 seconds is well worth learning, giving people bite-sized, easily shareable chunks of your knowledge.

Apps such as WordSwag and Flipagram allow you to do something outside the norm as well; for example, overlaying an image with a quotation or creating a short slideshow of a number of still photos. Anything that sticks out in someone's timeline has a better chance of grabbing their attention and, if you've spent the necessary time and effort building the relationship, even more likely.

This is based on personal experience.

As well as your own followers on Instagram, you also have the option to add hashtags to your posts. It is well worth investigating online which hashtags are appropriate for what you're trying to achieve and the audience you're trying to reach. *Lots* of users constantly search hashtags for posts of interest to them and it is a great way of attracting new followers.

Facebook

For clarity:

Facebook profile = your personal presence on Facebook
Facebook page = your business's presence on Facebook
Facebook group = a place set up so that people with a
    shared interest can congregate, outside of their own
    timelines; groups can be open (visible to everyone and
    anyone can post), closed (visible to everyone and only
    the members can post) or secret (invisible to everyone
    but the members)

As I write, Facebook has got engagement absolutely sorted. This is where a lot of the chat and conversation is now taking place, this is where people have moved so much of their online activity and, in late 2015, this is fast becoming somewhere where video is native.

As I have written a couple of books, my personal Facebook profile is open, so that anyone can see my posts, and I tend to accept most incoming friend requests. I also have a Facebook business page under my name, although I use that in a subtly different way.

Facebook is relationship building turbocharged. Slightly less fast moving than Twitter and yet still somewhere where the conversation is taking place, with or without you.

I use Facebook to build and engage with my crowd on several levels. I ensure I keep up to date with as many of my friends' timelines as possible. I like, comment on and share anything that I do genuinely like or think is worth sharing.

I post stuff about my interests and likes, such as Star Wars, rock music, rugby and the other things I like. I like how Facebook seems to like me sharing my sense of humour, so I do that as much as possible too or when I think of something funny!

My crowd, my friends and followers on Facebook then don't seem to mind if I push the occasional blatant advert for my stuff, either the books or one of my events. I think the balance here is vital. I tend to unfollow or unfriend people who only ever plug their stuff on Facebook. It is more of a pub or bar atmosphere in Facebook rather than a market. So you don't mind your friend occasionally mentioning their work, if they normally take part in the banter and chat. You wouldn't put up with a friend who continually just wanted to talk about themselves.

I currently use secret Facebook groups to build community among my clients and to share with them "premium" content outside of what I share publicly. For example, people who have attended The Networking Retreat will be able to see new techniques and new speakers who have been part of the retreat since they attended, but I don't share that publicly.

My Facebook page – stefanthomas.biz – I use to gain followers who are interested in business networking. That has a much more businesslike feel, with a higher proportion of adverts.

I share articles and blogs on my Facebook page. Mainly things I have written, and also business networking-related content, which I believe my followers will be interested in.

As I write this, native video on Facebook has started to become much more important than ever before, with Facebook undoubtedly positioning itself as a video-sharing platform.

I use video blogging when I want to say something about networking or another business-related topic, and will treat that just as I would a blog or article, sending it straight to my Facebook page.

Once an article or video is on my Facebook page, I also share it on my profile.

The ability to pay to boost your content on Facebook is fast becoming a necessity, with Facebook increasingly "gearing" how many of your followers see your posts. Facebook is a business and wants other businesses to pay to advertise and not just to let their stuff share naturally or organically.

Paying to boost your business posts, either to make sure more of your friends and their friends see them or choosing a dedicated target audience outside of your friends and followers, does undoubtedly raise the profile of your posts.

This has proven really useful to me in boosting my position as a thought leader in business networking. The ability, which Facebook affords me, for a very low fee, to put my blogs, articles and videos in front of people who would otherwise not have heard of me is a massive opportunity.

I create what I believe to be very valuable and useful content. If you do the same, then it is worth getting to know your way around Facebook ads and using them to build your presence. This is way too big a subject to sensibly cover in one chapter in this book. I recommend you find, using your network, a trusted adviser who can help you with Facebook ads. Talk to the people in your network about what results they've had, and, if their results have been spectacular, hunt down who is advising them and use them too.

YouTube

YouTube is where you allow people to get to know you. Outside of your writing and your Facebook posts, this is where people can see what you look like, what you sound like and how knowledgeable you appear when they watch you on film.

Think about this for a second. Two people provide the same service and one of those providers has video of them talking about the service, maybe even demonstrating how they implement that service. Someone searching for the service online finds the first provider with a nice website. They then find the second provider with a nice website, but this provider also talks directly to the person searching, through their videos. They actually start to build the vital rapport even before they ever talk to the prospect. They may even have provided some initial value by answering some of the questions the person searching may have had. The person searching now feels as though they "know" that provider; a huge step forward from just knowing their contact details and moving ever closer to that trust.

If you are speaking at an event, make sure someone is videoing you. It doesn't have to be professional quality; a modern smartphone will do the job until you can afford your own camera crew.

My own YouTube channel contains a mixture of videos other people have taken of me speaking, some professional video blogs I had commissioned with me in a "proper" studio, plus a load of stuff I have shot straight to my iPhone and uploaded there and then, mainly thoughts on networking and other business-related matters, particularly small business stuff.

I'm stunned by how simply I can now record, edit (using the onboard video editing tools on my phone) and upload my video to YouTube (and Facebook of course). That content is then searchable, viewable and shareable by the whole world. Whatever your passion is, you have the chance to talk about it to the wider world and, guess what, you will attract people who are interested in the same things as you, or searching for the answers to the questions you can help them to answer.

Allowing people to see what you look like and what you sound like can help to speed up the Meet–Like–Know–Trust really significantly. I have had people attend seminars who said to me that they came because "they already felt they knew me".

TIP: If you also use YouTube for family and personal stuff, then do set up a channel for your business to direct people to. I'm a big believer in being yourself on social, but if people come to your channel looking to be impressed by your expertise, they are unlikely to want to see your summer holiday videos.

Periscope

As I write, Periscope is still very much finding its way. Periscope, if you're not familiar with it, is a live streaming service, so after setting up the app on your phone, you can broadcast live to as many people in the world as are watching at the time.

Periscope, while being a video app, is nothing like YouTube. With YouTube you record something for people to watch; with Periscope you go live and you're there, talking to your viewers.

And, of course, they are talking back to you as well because a huge part of Periscope is the engagement by way of viewers being able to type comments live for you to reply to.

The opportunity here, in my opinion, to show off your expertise by being able to roll with the questions and answer them is huge. Periscope is ridiculously fast moving, so dealing with the questions as they come can be exhausting, but really worthwhile.

Also, if you have a business that is immersive, which people need to be able to see, then regular periscopes of what you do are very valuable to give people a "day in the life of"-type view of your work.

If you're a public speaker, then Periscope is a gift. Inviting people to 'scope your public presentations gives you the opportunity to build a bigger audience instantly. Make sure you invite people to follow you on your other social media channels as well.

I've watched a number of other people's 'scopes, as well as doing my own, and here is what I reckon wins on this relatively new platform:

1. Help people by giving them a time to watch you and stick to it – I have a regular show, which goes out at 8:30pm on a Monday for half an hour. I also do some random stuff through the week but that regular show gets, by far, the biggest audience. Instead of just hoping that people will be available to watch me, those people who want to are able to schedule it in.

2. Make sure you set Periscope to let your Twitter followers know you are going live *and* read Richard Eaton's excellent tip for getting more viewers here – "How to quadruple your Periscope audience". When people follow you on other platforms, they have already bought into you. Make sure you tweet and Facebook that you are going live at a particular time and then tweet and Facebook the link as you go live.

3. Have a plan for each 'scope. When I go live on Monday nights I have a card somewhere within my eyeline with some topic headlines on it. I prepare it in advance, often based on questions people have asked me about networking during the week. That way, I don't have to run out of things to say or dry up; I always know what the next topic is.

4. *Stop* thinking about it as a broadcast. People can, and do, interact by typing their comments in. The engagement factor on Periscope can be huge if you use it right. Far too often I watch people ignoring the comments and questions at the bottom that people have spent time typing. I get *far* more engagement by running each 'scope as a conversation, answering the questions in real time.

5. Give people a reason to keep coming back. Everyone has limited time so you need to make sure that they get real value from your 'scopes. Think about your content just as you would in a blog, podcast or video blog. Currently, people have pretty much unlimited choice what they watch and listen to.

I now really enjoy my 'scopes. I also keep my Twitter feed in front of me on my Chromebook as I get some questions coming in on Twitter for people who are watching the 'scope in a browser rather than on an app.

I have seen some really imaginative uses of Periscope. Remember, as with every social media platform, engagement and quality content are vital.

Content marketing

By the time you read this, I hope that "content marketing" is a term you are very familiar with. If not, it's another description for what you might have previously called blogging or article writing.

Content marketing is your ability to engage with your audience in longer, usually better written blogs, articles and white papers than the micro blogging platforms such as Twitter.

Your blogs and articles are somewhere where you must point your crowd to by sharing them on your other social media channels, but content marketing also gives you the chance to widen your audience by crafting your articles so that people find you from searches on Google and Bing.

I use my articles and blogs to educate people on various business networking topics. In order to do so, I try to answer questions that I've been asked in person because guess what? If someone is asking a question out in the real world, there are likely hundreds of people asking the same question of Google, Bing or the other search engines.

Content marketing is a massively valuable way to speed up the Meet–Like–Know–Trust. Think about it like this. If someone has met you at a networking event, or engaged with you on social, they will have some idea what you do from your networking introduction or your social profile. You can then demonstrate to them, by the quality of your articles and blogs, that you really do know what you're talking about.

I have built a reputation in the business networking arena by making sure that I continually and regularly educate my audience. I give them valuable content at no charge at all to them, except for their time. And if they take up some of their valuable time to comment on or share my articles, then I make sure I thank them for that.

The creation of valuable content is something that you can use to set yourself apart in a crowded and noisy marketplace. The creation of valuable content can make sure that people notice you over and above your competitors. The creation of valuable content can be the thing that means that people will talk to you first when they need to pay for your services.

Think about the people who are typing questions about your industry or profession into Google or Bing. How do you think they will feel about you and your business if you are the person answering those questions – for free?

What questions do people often ask in your marketplace? What worries them before they make a purchase? What excites them enough to want to make a purchase? What common misconceptions are there about your profession that people *always* ask about?

Imagine a world where almost every time someone asked a question of Google or Bing your website was the answer?

People very often tell me that they don't know what to blog about, but it is ridiculously simple.

Here's a really simple exercise to get you started.

Write down seven questions that people often ask you about your business.

Still stuck for ideas? Do people ask about cost? Do they ask about likely problems they will encounter? Do they ask what the difference is between this sort of service and that sort of service?

Do I need a solicitor or will writer?
How much does it cost to use an estate agent in YOURTOWN?
What if my financial adviser goes out of business?
What happens if my buyers pull out?
Who are the best website designers in YOURTOWN?
Should I have a WordPress website?
How much does training cost?

Every question needs an answer and you can put yourself in the position of being the person who answers people's questions online. I promise you that those same people, if you are talking to them online, will pick up the phone and talk to you.

Imagine coming across the most helpful service that answered all of your questions straightforwardly and honestly. What would you think of them? Be that service.

The other and vitally important part of this is that Google *loves* websites that are relevant to the questions people are asking. People will find you and once they've found you, of course, the conversation has started.

One hint that I picked up along the way is to add a footer to each and every one of your blog posts or articles, briefly explaining who you are and what you do, with relevant links embedded. That way you are making it easy for people to find you and buy from you.

Also, intersperse your blogs and articles with day-to-day advice and hints and tips for your audience. Stuff that they can pick up and use straight away.

I wrote earlier about building your reputation as an authority in your field by becoming someone who speaks about your subject. Writing articles and blogging is yet another way to build that reputation, particularly because, in the social media world, if your articles are "good", and you've done your groundwork and assembled your crowd, you are likely to find that they are shared by your network too.

Email marketing *is not* dead

I firmly believe in the premise of making it easy for people to find and digest your content in a way that is appropriate to them.

That's why I don't rely on people just finding my articles online. I maintain an email list of opted-in subscribers who have chosen to receive my emails and I regularly (weekly) email them to make sure they know where my latest blogs and articles are and keep gently in touch with them.

I personally use MailChimp (other email marketing software is available) because I happen to like the interface and the way it integrates with some of the other tools I use.

I make my emails conversational. I make no pretence that they aren't a circular, but I encourage people to reply, to let me know their recent networking successes and challenges and, really flatteringly, people do.

My emails don't attempt to oversell what I'm doing, although I'm not shy of popping the occasional link and reminder in there.

I use emails as simply another communication method, ensuring that those people who may want to read my articles have the opportunity to do so without having to hunt them down.

Currently, I'm getting open rates of over 30% on my emails, which I understand to be pretty good compared to the average. I put that down to making sure that my emails are, and have the reputation of being, crammed full of useful and valuable content.

TIPS:

- Get an email list; so many people don't and it's an opportunity wasted. Use professional email marketing software such as MailChimp or one of the many others. Don't attempt to cut corners and do it directly from Outlook or Google Mail. BCC (blind carbon copy) emails suck.
- Only ever subscribe people who know they're being subscribed. Ask people and respect if they don't want to be added.
- Send content regularly. Use this as another way of keeping in touch with people in a regular and meaningful way.
- Make your content as valuable as you possibly can. So that people look forward to reading it.
- Don't stress about unsubscribes. Even if your best friend unsubscribes. It's 2016 and it's what people do;

not everyone has the time to read your stuff no matter how valuable you know it is.

It's the people who don't unsubscribe and who genuinely read and digest your content who are moving closer to you and may well buy from you, when you have something they need, want and can afford.

Repurposing

Now here's a word I wish I'd learned many years ago, it would have saved me so much time.

To repurpose is to "adapt for use in a different purpose".

What that means in practice is that I take one piece of content and use it in my articles, which I then publish on my own blog as well as LinkedIn and Medium, plus I will often record a video to YouTube on the same subject, plus I will add that subject to my next Periscope broadcast, plus I will use pretty much the same text in my email that week. I will also share links to that content on my Facebook page and profile, and in my Twitter feed.

To put it simply, if you're already sending email newsletters, publish the same content in a blog; if you're already blogging, email that stuff out there. Whatever you're doing also record it as a YouTube or podcast.

Keeping track of your content

I use a simple editorial calendar to keep track of my content.

My editorial calendar is a simple spreadsheet that has a column for the date, a column for the title of the content and then separate columns to track where I have used and shared that content.

It is useful to brainstorm once a month and at least get the titles of your content down on the calendar, with a deadline for writing them. This gives you a significant advantage in trying to come up with content every week, which can often feel overwhelming. Plus, if you have a plan, you are less likely to let other stuff get in the way.

Plan your article writing and content creating into your diary in the same way you would your networking activity. Ensure that you make time for it, because it is an important, if not vital, part of your networking activity too.

Social media and content marketing play such an important role in our ongoing relationships with our business contacts. Ignoring social is, in my opinion, exceptionally dangerous for any business in the 21st century. Ignoring content marketing is becoming increasingly as dangerous. Putting in the effort to get it "right" is what people respond to. Effort in building relationships has always been valued in business. The methods of communication may be constantly changing, but the value that effort brings remains.

8
Standing out on LinkedIn

I was late to the party as far as LinkedIn is concerned. I was a refusenik for far too long, sticking to the social media platforms I personally preferred, such as Facebook and Twitter.

I've been using LinkedIn seriously for about three years now and am a convert. I can now track a significant proportion of my sales back to my activity on LinkedIn.

Using LinkedIn should become a part of your networking activity too. The same disciplines apply, growing your network and then keeping regularly in contact with that network.

Think of LinkedIn as an extension of your networking activity in the real world.

Something that you should do regularly is ensure that your LinkedIn profile is up to date, and is designed to help people find you, if they're looking for someone with your skills.

Your LinkedIn profile is completely editable, so think about what you should put in there.

The headline is what appears next to your name on every post and update you share. It is also searchable. So what should you put in there?

Many people simply have their official title and name of their company, which isn't helpful if people are quickly looking at your update and trying to work out what you do.

Your headline should make it easy for people to instantly understand what you offer.

For example, if mine was set as my official title and company name it would read:

"Stefan Thomas. Director. No Red Braces Training Ltd."

Helpful? Not.

Instead it reads:

"Stefan Thomas – Trainer, Speaker & Coach | Author of Amazon Bestseller Business Networking For Dummies | Business Networking Expert"

Instantly, anyone spotting my posts or updates can see what I do and anyone searching for what I do can easily find it.

When people view your profile, your work history appears underneath the headline anyway, so that information is covered.

Your "Summary" then gives you the chance to expand a little on what you do and how you work. Think very hard about the words you want to be found for as, once again, this is searchable.

A tip that I was given is to use a word cloud generator, which will graphically show you which words are used most often and therefore have the most "weight" in any piece of text you put together. Several exist on the Internet as free services, just Google "word cloud generator" and find one that suits you.

When you've drafted your text, drop it into the word cloud generator. Are the biggest words the ones you expected? The words people are likely to be searching for if you want them to find you? If not, rewrite and rewrite again until you get it right.

Underneath the summary, you can add any media, such as videos of you speaking, photos, whitepapers and any other documents you think would help people who have found your profile. I've got a few videos of me speaking, because speaking is one of the things I want people to find me for.

Once you are happy with your profile, you need to make it easy for people to connect with you on LinkedIn and to remind people that you exist.

Get into the habit of connecting on LinkedIn with everyone you meet at networking events. Download the LinkedIn app, which makes this really simple, as does Evernote, which you can use to scan business cards where it then magically finds that person on LinkedIn and sends them a connection request. You should extend this to anyone who offers you a card at an event.

You should also be open to accept most incoming connection requests, apart from those that are obviously spam. Avoid judging people by their title or nature of their business – you never know who they might be connected to, either now or in the future. I'm still genuinely flattered that anyone would want to connect with me, and treat my relationship with them accordingly.

Now you've got connections, it's worth making sure you are, once again, raising your profile as someone who knows your stuff and is an authority on your subject.

One of the biggest gifts that LinkedIn gives to its subcribers is that everything you post is designed to be viral.

All of my blog posts are also repurposed to LinkedIn posts. So whenever I post something on LinkedIn, it goes onto the timeline of my connections and followers.

The absolutely awesome thing about LinkedIn is that whenever one of your connections or followers likes or comments on one of your posts, that fact is then shared with their connections timelines – giving your posts a potentially massive audience.

As with any platform, LinkedIn prefers native content, so I strongly advocate repurposing your blogs as posts on LinkedIn rather than simply sharing a link, which would be an update.

For example, you might use posts on LinkedIn to educate and give value to your connections and followers, and updates for anything that is close to being promotional or an ad.

My recommendation is for anyone to publish at least two posts per week on LinkedIn, along with regular updates as well. This keeps you accessible and visible.

One of the biggest and often overlooked opportunities on LinkedIn is that it actively tells you when there is something of interest to one of your connections, which you could comment on.

When you log onto LinkedIn in a browser, as opposed to one of the apps, up in the top right-hand corner you will see a box that says "XX ways to keep in touch". When you look at that, you will see that it shares significant events in your connections' lives, such as a new business venture or title, or the fact that they have been in business for so many years.

Once again, this is simply an excuse for you to be in touch with that connection, on their turf, in a way that is interesting to them, and yet remind them at the same time that you exist.

So whenever you log onto LinkedIn (and I'd recommend you do this daily), consider checking the top right-hand corner first, before publishing anything yourself.

Regularly updating your profile is also a way of reminding people that you are there because every time you do so LinkedIn tells your network that you have updated your profile (assuming you have this option enabled).

Regularly posting interesting and useful articles on LinkedIn definitely boosts the number of people viewing your profile. If I am ever too busy to post something on LinkedIn (when I'm writing a book, for example), my profile views and as a result my enquiries from LinkedIn drop like a stone. When I'm active on the platform my profile views and messages and connection requests rise exponentially.

Groups on LinkedIn

LinkedIn has groups that enable people with a similar business interest to discuss that and communicate within that group.

Note that the people in the group might not immediately be connections of yours, but you can still enter into discussions with them.

In LinkedIn, go to "Interests" and then "Groups" and start to search out groups that are of interest to you, then join.

Some groups are hopelessly sparse, it appears that whoever set up the group ran out of enthusiasm very shortly after doing so, but some are very active, with extremely robust and vibrant discussions going on.

Remember that every single time you post a reply, or get stuck into a discussion, your name and your headline, linking to your profile, appear next to whatever you post, giving you and your articles and posts even more visibility.

Searching and connecting

As much as you want people to be able to find you, LinkedIn also gives you the chance to find and connect directly with the people you want to talk to.

NOTE: I am basing this on being a Premium rather than Free member of LinkedIn, which in my opinion is a worthwhile investment.

Right at the top of your LinkedIn screen is a "Search" box that enables you to search for people by name, job title, company, or any other keywords, including the ones in your headline.

If you really want to get in touch with someone, then find them using this facility. Then, before you go any further, read their profile and do a little bit of research. That way, when you do send them a message, you will at least be able to personalize it a little rather than just sending a bland, copy and pasted message. If you are a Premium member of LinkedIn, their profile will also reveal to you a "Contact Info" tab that, if they have filled it in, will have such things as their Twitter handle and other contacts.

As with any social platform, LinkedIn is about respecting not only the platform, but the members there as well.

LinkedIn continues to evolve and develop and most businesses and business owners don't make enough effort to really make the most of the platform. I hope that some of the hints and tips in here have helped you to take it forward. Simply being on there isn't enough. Being on there and regularly using the platform to keep in touch with your network will make a difference. Being on there, regularly using the platform and delivering value to your network will make even more of a difference.

9
Joining it all up

Much of your networking success is going to come from learning to join all of this up. When you apply all of this, you can truly dominate your networking environment and social media for your business. Remember that you're generating opportunities and, as someone once said, "when opportunity knocks, you still have to get up off your arse and open the door ... ".

Say yes to every opportunity

An awful lot of the opportunities I am offered along the way come with no immediate payday. I am asked to speak for free, to appear on podcasts and guest blog for other people.

Gary Vaynerchuk sums it up beautifully when he says that "1>0". Whatever you're doing, you are constantly pushing yourself and your business forward and reminding people that you exist.

I put myself out there on social media and talk about business networking a lot. As a result of that, I am flattered when people connect with me and engage with me. About a year or so ago as I write this, I was contacted by Kevin Willett, who runs networking events and speaks about networking a lot over in New Hampshire, USA.

After chatting for a while on Twitter, Kevin asked if I would appear on his "Friends of Kevin" radio show. So, late one night, over Skype, I chatted to Kevin and his audience about networking.

Was there any immediate benefit to me in doing this? Well, yes as it happens, because I needed experience of being interviewed on radio and Kevin was a fantastic host, so I've been able to use that experience with the radio and TV interviews I've done since.

But nobody paid me for that time – so what was the point?

That interview lives on with a link from my blog. It regularly gets shared and retweeted. And I've no idea who will listen to it, now or in the future.

Every opportunity is an opportunity and *none* of them come with labels to tell you which ones are going to pay off financially and immediately and which ones aren't.

I have been going to The Business Show in London twice a year, for the whole two days every time, every year since 2007. At first I was an attendee, then I helped out on the 4Networking stand and became part of the crowd there.

And at no point did anyone pay me.

In June 2013 I was at the after-party and sat next to the person who turned out to be a commissioning editor for "The Dummies" series of books, which is how I ended up being asked to write *Business Networking For Dummies*.

And nowadays I am a keynote speaker at The Business Show, due, in no small part, to me turning up and treating it constantly as an opportunity to build my network and become part of the crowd at the show, whereas others decided it was too far to travel or too much like hard work.

Seize every opportunity to grow and develop your network, no matter how small or insignificant that opportunity appears at the time.

If you want to win referrals, you need to do this too

One of the questions people ask me a lot is "how do I get more referrals from my networking?"

After all, that is why a lot of people first attend networking events, first to see if there are people in the room who will buy from them and second to see if the people in the room know people outside the room who will buy from them.

We talk a lot about building up the Meet–Like–Know–Trust, that process whereby people go from their first ever handshake with you, to having enough confidence in you to refer you to their best client. I maintain that process isn't bound to time, but immersion – it doesn't need to take six months or a year to build that trust, if you spend enough time in contact with the other people in a meaningful way.

By "meaningful" I am suggesting that you always give value first in your relationships.

But there is one thing you must do. One thing that can speed up the process. One thing that can lead to many more referrals.

And that is to put your heart and soul into what you do and the service you provide to your clients, and be demonstrably brilliant at it.

Networking and social media are an absolute gift if you're working with people and thrilling them with the astonishing quality of what you do and the value that you give. People *want* to boast if they've bought well, if they've paid for something and been absolutely thrilled with the value they received. That's what we do. If I buy from someone else and I am impressed, I always mention that on Facebook and LinkedIn, tagging the person or business I refer to.

The thing with putting every effort into being outstanding is that clients are reasonable when things don't quite work, when it does rain on your parade.

As well as putting the effort into building the relationships, as well as networking with a passion, make sure that your clients can see how brilliant you are so that they can tell people.

Doing a weekly audit of your networking

Who did you have a one to one with last Wednesday? Can you still remember? Did you promise to do anything? To send an email or make an introduction to someone else? Have you done it?

What about that one to one you had three months ago. Can you remember anything about it? Particularly if you regularly attend networking events and have lots of one to ones.

Here's something I recommend.

Every week, audit your networking for the previous week. Go back through your memory, the business cards you've collected and, if you're a member of 4Networking, the "View Attendees" feature of the 4N website for the meetings you've been to.

Have a good think about those conversations you had. If you've read *Business Networking For Dummies* you'll know that I strongly recommend taking notes and actions immediately after the event. But sometimes it doesn't happen. So think about those conversations you had last week. Did you make any notes? Is there anything you said you were going to do that you haven't done yet?

By the way, I'm a massive fan of Evernote and use it to scan in business cards and make notes on them (something I recommend in the book). I also use a CRM system called Capsule to make sure that I record everything and set myself tasks to follow up with people, so that I don't forget.

Here's the thing: I have said very often that "Every big opportunity starts with a little conversation." It's vital that you take action on those little conversations. Who mentioned that they are "thinking about" coming to your next workshop? Or might be interested in you working with them "at some point"? Are you going to rely on them doing something about it, or will you gently follow up with them and keep in touch with them so that you are in the right place at the right time when they are ready to do something about it?

Sit down once a week and reflect on the little conversations you've had that week. Was there something you were meant to do? And, more importantly, did someone move a little closer to you and are you taking the actions necessary to give that some momentum?

PS: This is part of what I do when I am coaching someone. I make sure we pick every little detail out of their conversations so they get maximum value from their networking. It's astonishing how many little opportunities most people miss along the way that, if followed up, turn into actual business.

You've got a level playing field, now go out there and play

For so long, small business owners would complain that there was no level playing field. The bigger companies had the bigger marketing budget and the bigger opportunities to promote themselves.

It wasn't fair, how could a small business possibly compete with that?

And then, in the early part of the 21st century, someone invented the level playing field. Modern business networking, content marketing and social media gave businesses, no matter how big or small, the same chance to promote themselves.

All of a sudden, businesses of any size could get themselves out there and start connecting with potential customers anywhere in the world.

And yet, most of them still don't. Most of them remain passive, waiting aggressively for the phone to ring.

And that is where the opportunity lies. Because if you are the person who will put yourself out there, and connect, engage, and promote relentlessly and with a passion that befits your business, then you will be miles ahead of your competition, and you will instantly see your network develop, profitably.

A second chance to make a first impression

I can be a pedant too and I realize that my heading apparently makes no sense. Of course, you can only make one first impression because anything after that, by definition, isn't the first. I get that.

But what I also realize is that loads of people in sales and in business get tied up with this idea that you only ever get one chance. And because of that, they never ever try for a second chance to make an impression, if the first try didn't go according to plan.

People have been told so often, in every branch of sales and business training, that "you only get one chance to make a first impression" that it discourages them from one of the most important lessons, in my opinion, in business. You can *always* get up, dust yourself off, and try again.

And in business networking you *always* get a second chance to make a first impression.

Think about this. If I was trying to sell to you in the real world and cold called you, how long would I get to make an impression (presuming you took the call in the first place)? And if that first call didn't go well, if I didn't convince you to do business or listen to me further, how far would I get if I called a second time? At the very least I would have to make a massive effort to convince you to listen again.

But at a business networking event, if my 40-second introduction didn't work this time, I can simply go home and work on another. If nobody wants to find out more about what I do, that's cool, it is actually really useful information that my first approach didn't work. So I can come back next week and try a second approach, and then a third and then a fourth.

Not only does business networking put you directly in front of the people who might do business with you, or refer business to you, it also gives you a massive opportunity to constantly refine and improve your approach.

You should treat networking as a continuous journey. Every setback is actually a valuable lesson. Every meeting has value, whether or not you secure a new client.

One of the things I truly love about networking is that it's the only sales environment I've ever been in where you get a second chance, and unlimited chances, to make a first impression.

It doesn't actually matter if your 40-second introduction this morning sucked. You can go back and do it tomorrow.

You didn't manage to have a conversation with the person you really wanted to speak to at the event? No problem, you have something in common now and an excuse to call them and tell them exactly why you would have loved a conversation and get it scheduled.

Networking offers you a second chance to make a first impression. It is up to you to take those chances, and I sincerely hope you will.

Please do keep me up to date with your networking journey and your successes along the way.

One of the fantastic things about networking and social media is that most people won't bother to put the effort in to really make it work. You've taken the time to read this book, now please take the time to make it work for you.

Thank you.

Further Reading

Here are the books I mention at various points throughout *Instant Networking*:

Carnegie, Dale, *How to Win Friends and Influence People*, 2006, ISBN 0091906814.

Jeffers, Susan, *Feel the Fear and Do It Anyway: How to Turn Your Fear and Indecision into Confidence and Action*, 2007, ISBN 0091907071.

Thomas, Stefan, *Business Networking For Dummies*, 2014, ISBN 111883335X.

Vaynerchuk, Gary, *Crush It!: Why NOW is the Time to Cash in on your Passion*, 2013, ISBN 0062295020.

About the Author

Stefan Thomas first walked into a business networking meeting in late 2005, and hated it.

He found it terrifying. The thought of walking up to people he didn't know and engaging in small talk and then, worse, having to stand up in front of a room full of people and talk about his business was all way out of his comfort zone.

Over time though, he worked out that this networking might actually work and, after a change in circumstances in 2007, threw himself into networking with brute force. Desperation, rather than any particular strategy meant that Stefan had to work out how to make this work commercially, so he did.

His reputation as someone who knew how to make networking work, for any business owner, started to grow and in 2012, Stefan was asked to become a Director of 4Networking Ltd, helping to steer the network out of an incredibly turbulent period and turning it round into the successful joined up network it is today.

In 2014 Stefan's first book *Business Networking for Dummies* was published, which has sold thousands of copies across the world and established Stefan as the leading authority on business networking in the 21st century.

Leaving 4Networking in 2015 to concentrate on his own business – The Networking Retreat – Stefan can now be found speaking at conferences and events all over the UK, to business audiences of all sizes, and from all business sectors.

Stefan is very active on social media and welcomes connections from his readers

on Twitter – twitter.com/noredbraces
on Facebook – facebook.com/stefanthomas/biz
and on LinkedIn – uk.linkedin.com/in/noredbraces

Acknowledgements

I couldn't possibly name everyone who has contributed to this book. The list includes everyone I have met whilst networking, as well as everyone who I've met who has told me why networking doesn't work.

Every conversation has helped me to learn a little bit more and to put together the ideas and strategies you find in this book.

The team at Wiley have, as ever, been superb in guiding me through the writing process, so thank you to Vicky Kinsman and the team there, once again.

The Directors of 4Networking Ltd, Brad Burton, Terry Cooper and Jason Dutton deserve a mention for continuing to build the platform from which I learnt so much.

And, of course, to those people who believed in me during my journey, and continue to do so now. To try to name them would risk leaving someone out.

Notes

Notes

Notes

Notes

Notes